Publish Smart

How to Harness the Power of New Technology to Grow Your Creative Empire

The Creative Entrepreneur Series

Beth Ann Erickson

Publish Smart

How to Harness the Power of New Technology to Grow Your Creative Empire

The Creative Entrepreneur Series

Beth Ann Erickson

Publish Smart

Introduction

There's only one reason to become a writer. One reason and one reason only. We'll talk about why you write later. First, we have a few technicalities to discuss....

I became a freelance writer with a dream in my heart and rose-colored glasses firmly in place. With dreams of wildly creative mornings and lazy afternoons, I began sending out queries to the "lucrative" magazine markets while slaving over my "Great American Novel."

And so I worked. And worked. And worked.

My first year of freelancing netted a whopping $1,000 (give or take) and more rejection letters than I could count.

To make matters worse, not one person I contacted asked to review my first novel.

To call that period of my life "frustrating" would be an understatement.

But I didn't give up. I decided to research my craft and learn everything I could about the business of publishing. I discovered that with just a little change in my focus, I could work smarter, not harder. Doing this increased my acceptance rate to around 90 percent.

This book contains much of what I learned these past few years… information that'll make your transition from someone who writes to "published author."

Best of luck always, and keep in touch. You can always contact me at FilbertPublishing.com.

~~ Beth

Inside This Book

Step One: Choose Your Options Carefully ~~ 7
Step Two: Educate Yourself... Get Really Good at
Persuasion ~~ 18
Step Three: Contacting Publishers/Markets and Mastering
the Craft ~~ 40
Power Persuasion ~~ 41
Ten Steps to Freelancing Freedom ~~ 49
Beyond the Writer's Market: Lucrative Assignments in
any Economy ~~ 64
How to Write, Publish, and Sell Profitable Books – a Self
Publishing Primer ~~ 75
Sample Zine ~~ 97
Sample Publishing Agreement ~~ 106
Conclusion ~~ 112

Step One: Choose Your Options Carefully

Let's begin by talking about book publishers. Don't worry, if you're into the magazine market, we'll get there in a minute. Much of what we're about to discuss applies to both short and long manuscripts.

Because this section isn't intended to be an exhaustive study of various types of publishers, my intent here is to give you a general overview of the industry so you'll know how to target your efforts and increase your chances for success.

The Big Wigs

I'll bet you didn't know that there are only around five major book publishers world-wide. Yup. Just five.

Now, these major companies have a gazillion subsidiaries, enough to create a pretty big dent in the annual "Writer's Market."

What does this mean to you?

It means that unless you've got a pretty big portfolio, unless you've got a great deal of success under your belt, unless you're a fairly big name, your chances of cracking into this market is pretty small. Not impossible... just small.

Big publishers tend to eye profitability and marketability as major contributors determining whether they'll accept a book for publication.

Big publishing houses receive thousands of unsolicited manuscripts and queries each week. Unless you have an inside contact in the house, the chances your query/manuscript will receive any attention whatsoever is slim.

If a big publisher accepts your manuscript, you can expect a small advance and can earn between a 6% to 10% royalty based on the net receipts. For example, if your $20 book wholesales for $10, you'd receive between .60 and $1.00 per book sold based on this type of arrangement.

Beware... some writers have complained that their books never earned back their "advance on royalties" and were asked to return some of their advance. Other writers never earned anything beyond their advance. Be aware of this situation and carefully read any contract before you sign it.

But I digress....

If you aren't a celebrity, don't expect much promotional effort put into your book. Publishers tend to follow the 80/20 rule... 80 percent of their promo dollars go into the top 20 percent of their books. The remaining 20 percent of their promo dollars go into 80 percent of their titles.

Also, you can expect that your book will be available for between 6 months and one year. After that it'll be "remaindered" into discount bins.

If you've signed your rights away, this may spell the end of your book. Sometimes the rights to your book may revert to you after the contract ends, sometimes they don't.

Read your contract carefully if you ever hope to own your manuscript again.

Medium and Small Publishers

Medium and small publishers generally serve a niche and often have a built-in audience for that market.

For example, Filbert Publishing specializes in publishing books for creative entrepreneurs: freelance writers, small business owners, musicians, poets, etc. Using Writing Etc. (our free e-mag for our target audience) as a big part of our promo plan, we're able to effectively sell these types of titles to our readers. We also publish some fiction... after all, writers tend to be voracious readers.

However, give us a book about fishing, and we'd be sunk (no pun intended). We like to stick to our specialty and our authors know this.

Don't expect much of an advance from a small and medium publisher. Many don't give advances at all.

With a strong, targeted book proposal, you're almost assured to receive an educated read from the people at many of these houses. This is assuming, of course, that you've researched the publishing house and have sent them appropriate material.

For example, although Filbert Publishing publishes books for creative entrepreneurs, I'd venture to guess that one query out of 200 is targeted to our readership. We've received books on every subject under the sun… with the rare queries pitching a book for the audience we'd like to serve.

If other publishing houses mirror mine (and I hear they do) consider the success you can have when all your queries are tightly targeted.

Which leads me to my next point: read any contract you may be offered carefully. Find out if your royalty schedule is based on the retail price of the book (this is best) or "net receipts" (not as good), or "net profits" (you don't want this). More about this in the "Red Flag" section of this book.

Your book will enjoy a longer life at a medium to small publisher, many times your book will live on as long as you'd like it to.

You won't pay fees of any kind at a legitimate publishing house. If they begin asking for money for any reason, politely pull out of the negotiations.

When you contact a small or medium sized publisher, do your homework. Order a couple of their books and see what they look like. Are they full of errors? What do the covers look like? Will they produce something you can be proud of?

Thoroughly research their current title list, their submission guidelines, and read through their contract. If they appear to be someone you'd like to work with, contact them.

Subsidy, Vanity, and Predatory Publishing

Not many publishing houses will fess up to being a subsidy or vanity house. A ton of new terms have popped up in an attempt to remove the stigma of "subsidy/vanity publisher" on their label.

You can easily spot one of these "publishers" by asking yourself one question:

* Does this company charge me money to get published?

* Does this company demand that I purchase a set number of books or they won't publish my manuscript?

If the answer's "Yes" to either of these questions, then they're more than likely a subsidy publisher and you'd do best to avoid them.

To get legitimately published, you shouldn't have to provide the publishing company with any money. Period. Ever.

A legit house will lay out, edit, design, and help you promote the book, everything... for free... because they believe your book will sell enough copies to recoup their investment.

After all, if your publisher doesn't believe your book will sell, why would you allow them to publish it?

You need a publisher who believes in your project lock, stock, and barrel... and is willing to invest the time and money in promoting it correctly.

Bottom line: Unless you plan on self publishing your work, never pay even one red cent to get your work published.

Subsidy and vanity publishers don't have a good reputation in the book selling business. If your book holds their label, you'll have a very difficult time selling it to anyone beyond your local community.

But, things could be worse. If you tangle with a predatory publishing company, chances are slim to none that you'll find your project turning a profit. Here's an example:

I once witnessed a company with a very good reputation adopt predatory publishing methods. It began innocently enough when they launched a self publishing mentoring program costing close to ten grand. During this period, the mentorees wrote their book, paid for editing, purchased great covers, created marketing plans... they did everything a solid self publisher does. Then, the mentorees could "apply" to become an author under the mentor's publishing house.

Long story short, these authors paid for everything. Then they paid a giant fee to get considered for what appeared to be a more traditional publishing opportunity, but it wasn't. Then they signed contracts allowing this once reputable company to take a cut of all profits for… who knows how long? Some contracts never have a sundown clause.

Most frustrating? This company has a waiting list for their mentor program.

You can avoid this scam by remembering that money always flows towards the writer, not away.

POD

POD is the latest buzzword in the publishing biz. Actually, POD has been around for a long time.

POD stands for "Print On Demand." In the past, this term has been used to describe the use of new printing equipment capable of printing one book at a time.

For example, a customer orders a book, miles away, a huge machine prints one book, the book's shipped to the bookstore (or directly to the customer), the customer happily reads.

The beauty of this system is that publishers don't have to pay for thousands of books to languish in their inventories while they wait to sell. Each book is sold as it is purchased.

Technically speaking, this business model should work. And it does. Sometimes.

After all, every book is (technically speaking again) printed "one at a time." Even in the days of scribes and monks, books were printed "one at a time."

However, a number of problems have cropped up with this new POD business model.

First, I need to clarify this "POD" term. "Print on Demand" has (for some unknown reason) evolved from focusing on this marvelous new technology to focusing on a few "publishers" who exploit this technology along with many unsuspecting authors.

Often, the term POD refers to a business model (rather than the printing technology) where virtually anyone can set up a "publishing house," contract with a company like Lightning Source (owned by Ingram) and Ingram Spark to print their books, and start selling.

Some of the biggest POD "publishing companies" today are Createspace, Lulu, Trafford, iUniverse, Bookbaby, Dog Ear Publishing, AuthorHouse, Xlibris and more.

Although there are definite benefits to having your book published by one of these companies... benefits like higher royalties when compared with traditional publishing houses, more control over your book edits, you don't have to go through any manuscript submission process... there are definite liabilities to this type of arrangement.

Your books will cost more. Where a traditional publishing house can order print runs large enough to keep their price per book at around a couple bucks per. Printing one book at these places will cost you between six and seven dollars... not counting postage to get it to the bookstore or customer.

Some of these companies will nickel and dime you on additional services like custom covers, editing, marketing, etc. You can easily spend tens of thousands of dollars just to get one title to press.

Your books will receive limited distribution. Yeah, they'll be available at nearly every online bookstore. But booksellers (the brick and mortar kind) are reluctant to order POD books. This happens because POD publishing companies are unable to reduce the wholesale price of the book to give bookstores a decent discount. Also, many POD titles re nonreturnable. This makes bookstores very hesitant to take a chance on an unknown author.

Then we have the discount problem. Many of these companies will not offer bookstores a deep enough discount to make your title profitable.

For example, a book retailing for 12.95 will be discounted 55 percent for the privilege of being stocked at a Baker and Taylor warehouse. Baker and Taylor (along with Ingram) is a major wholesaler of books… you need to get your book into one of these warehouses or you will not receive wide-spread distribution. Luckily, LightningSource as well as Ingram Spark are owned by Ingram and for a fee, will include your title in their database. But if even if your company provides a hefty discount (which they won't)... don't expect bookstore inclusion.

Here's a typical scenario:

Baker and Taylor warehouses your book until a few orders start coming in. After the orders arrive, they'll fill them and contact your publisher when they need more books.

But here's the hitch: a 55 percent discount on a $12.95 book equals a $7.12. This means your publisher earns 5.83 (minus postage to get the book to Baker and Taylor) for each book.

Subtract the author royalty and the profit margin gets slimmer.

If your POD book costs more than a couple dollars to print, your publisher could easily wind up in the hole profit wise.

So... that's why many POD publishers reduce the bookstore discount. It's a viscous cycle. Publishers need to make a profit so they short discount. That makes bookstores not purchase your book because they're in business to make money. (Go figure.)

They'll stick to stocking profitable books, squeezing your chances of obtaining a readership.

This scenario highlights why so many POD publishers charge their authors so many fees... they're in business to make money from selling to authors... not sell books.

But there are also other disadvantages going with a POD publisher:

Your book will not receive much pre-publication publicity. You simply sign a contract and, voila… you've got a book.

Traditional publishers take anywhere from six to 12 months to send out galleys to reviewers, obtain Library of

Congress numbers, send out press releases, and such. Often the lion's share of publicity occurs before the book even hits bookstores. You lose out on a lot of prepublication work when you blindly choose a POD publisher.

Another disadvantage? Sometimes you may wind up with an odd contract. Some POD contracts are incomplete, exploitative, and even abusive. Watch for no termination clauses, no rights reverting back to you, worldwide (long term) rights to your work, and terms changing without notice.

Here's a great resource you can use to compare various POD publishers:

http://booksandtales.com/pod/index.php

Be wary of the POD business model. From my experience, it's difficult to make a living as a writer with the terms many of these companies offer. Also, with little to no marketing assistance, many authors find themselves on their own. Customer service rarely involves more than cryptic emails. These types of businesses are evolving daily. Approach with caution.

Self Publishing

If you choose to self publish, you'll not only write your book, you'll need to work with editors, get it formatted, design the cover (or have someone do this for you), and deal directly with the printer to order as many copies as you'd like.

Depending on how you tackle this project, you'll foot the bill for all these tasks however in many cases heading out alone could save you tens of thousands of dollars.

When all your tasks are complete, your book should be indistinguishable from one produced by one of the big five.

You'll need to promote your title but you'll retain all the profits. Best of all, you'll maintain total control over your book.

Self publishing is a viable option if you have a strong entrepreneurial side of your personality. Gone are the days of rejection letters. Forget polishing the queries. You write, you upload files to your selected company, and move onto your next project.

Today your free time (what's that?) is spent nosing out new markets and making your new book a success.

That's the good news.

The not so great? Everybody and their brother is striving to become the next Amazon Best Seller. Scams abound. Even purchasing books on the topic of publishing to Kindle is a crap shoot.

Courses on how to game the system pop up faster than corn in a microwave.

"Want to make a gazillion bucks using [insert the terms Amazon, Facebook, Twitter, or Google here] advertising? Buy my course!! Become the next JK Rowling!~!"

Yeah. Avoid stuff like that.

If you want to self publish, if writing flows in your blood, if you have something you really need to share... go for it. Write. Publish. Repeat. Don't give up.

Trite advice? Perhaps. But it works.

I've been at this since '95. Gimmicks come and go. The long term authors in this biz eschew the latest fad and keep writing. They build an audience. They keep in contact with them.

They never give up.

If you choose the self publishing option, be sure to research the process thoroughly. Read self publishing titles by people with a long term track record. Don't only market online, cultivate real world sales channels as well. Find self published authors with long term track records and mimic their methods.

Later on in this book, you can find out an exciting option available to self-published authors using the POD technology we just discussed. Examine the next section of this book carefully if you plan on self publishing. There's an exciting new world of printing options available to you.

And Then We Have Mags....

Perhaps you don't write long manuscripts but would rather focus on short fiction and articles. That's great. Thanks to the Internet, your options are wider and more varied than ever before.

A number of years ago I launched The Creative Mindset Newsletter. Each month, I created an eight page screed outlining marketing techniques, mindset information, and general entertainment. I charged $9.95 per issue. When someone subscribed, Paypal initiated a subscription that was deducted monthly.

It was an easy process. I wrote a new issue. Then as subscription fees trickled in, I'd pop the new issue in the local post box.

This project was easier than I expected. I loved my subscribers. It was fun to know I could depend on a certain portion of my income to land in my bank account each month.

Today, I could see how this process could easily be replicated electronically.

The cons? Constant promotion. But as far as cons go, that's actually pretty minor.

That said, if you don't want to become a publisher yourself, you can easily contribute to other people's publications.

Let's begin by clarifying a few things:

First, don't write for free. "Exposure" rarely works in your favor. You're a professional. Get paid for your craft.

Second, never pay to get published. Your mantra should always be, "Money flows towards the writer, not away."

Third, when you're targeting publications you'd like to write for, remember to start small. Smaller publications are more apt to read and respond to your query. Once you get published in the smaller markets, then you can target larger markets.

Fourth, don't forget online markets. E-magazines (or

electronic magazines) are hungry for content. Often they pay on acceptance so you can expect a check (or some money dumped in your Paypal account http://paypal.com) within days. Writers who don't trawl for online markets cheat themselves out of a lot of fun and a host of opportunities.

Fifth, watch what rights the magazine is purchasing. One-time rights are best. This means they're purchasing your article and will publish it once. First North American rights means they'll be the first organization in North America to publish your work. Exclusive, World-wide, or All Rights are detrimental to the writer. It's your article. Don't let a publication buy it outright and make it illegal for you to use it again.

To increase your chances of getting an acceptance letter from a publisher, target your query. Begin by reading a few issues of the magazine. You want to capture the tone of each issue. Study the language they use and mimic that tone in your article as well as your query. Now you need to get your hands on their writer guidelines.

After doing your background research, craft an awesome query and mail (or e-mail) it to the editor.

I'll discuss specific query techniques later on.

Now, you can target another magazine (or e-mag... you'll find a sample e-mag later in this book) and begin the whole process again. Decide how many queries you'd like to send out daily, then do it. Regular query writing will result in regular writing assignments.

Step Two: Educate Yourself

In this section, I'll discuss a few terms, procedures, and "frequently asked questions" I've run across as I've dug through the Writing Etc. e-mail. In this biz, it certainly pays to be an educated consumer. The more you know, the more profitable your business and the less likely you'll get scammed.

So, let's get to it, eh?

Publishing FAQs
Do I Need An Agent?

If you're a magazine writer, no.

If you write long fiction, the answer is, "Maybe."

I've had nine books published. None of them had an agent. In fact, I found a home for my first novel myself, a feat my agent couldn't seem to accomplish.

A good literary agent will match manuscripts with the right publisher. Often, they're the only way you'll break into the big New York publishing houses.

An agent will make manuscript suggestions, will negotiate your contract, and will keep their eye open for film rights, audio book rights, etc.

Unfortunately, roughly half (according to the Literary Agent's Marketplace) of all agents will not read manuscripts by unpublished authors. Expect 15 percent to not even reply to your query.

In fact, sometimes it's harder for a new writer to get a good agent than a publisher.

If an agent you've contacted has said they're interested in your manuscript and will read the whole thing for a fee, you can be assured that this agent isn't legit. Stop all communication with them.

If an agent says they'll represent you if you get your manuscript edited... usually by someone they recommend... don't sign any agreement with them.

A common scam in the literary agent community is to

receive kick-backs from editors when they send them work. If an agent recommends a particular editor, it's highly likely they'll receive cash for the recommendation and you'll receive a (somewhat) edited manuscript, but no representation in the end.

As always, money should always flow towards the writer, not away.

How much money can I expect to make if I get something published?

This depends on a number of factors.

According to AbsoluteWrite.com, the average freelance wage is around $4,000 per year. Yup. You read right. Four grand.

David Morrell in his book Lessons From A Lifetime of Writing is a bit more optimistic. He says the number's around $6,500 per year.

About now you're probably thinking: But what about the huge advances I hear big name authors are getting?

Morrell tells us that he received $85,000 for the paperback rights for his novel First Blood.

Sounds great, huh?

Here's the breakdown:

He had to share half that fee with his original publisher, the one who published the hard cover version of the book. Cha ching: he's down $42,500 leaving $42,500 for him.

Then he had to subtract 10 percent for his agent's fee ($4,250) leaving him with $38,250.

Combined federal and state income taxes snared $15,300 leaving him with $22,950… a far cry from 85 grand for this respected writer of such novels as Rambo, Fraternity of the Stone, and Covenant of the Flame. So, in his case 22k was a far cry from 85k.

It is possible to make a living as a writer. But you'll probably have to diversify into other avenues of writing to make that living wage.

Some writing assignments you can use to supplement your

income in a big way include:

* Newspaper writing
* Writing for e-mags
* Magazine writing
* Writing a column
* Editing
* Publishing
* Writing advertising copy
* Write direct mail

Writing opportunities are limited only by your imagination. Yeah... you just may write your Great American Novel... but in the mean time, you can still write and make a living at it. You may even get rich in the process. But guaranteed, you'll sure have a lot of fun.

How Do I Contact a Publisher or Agent?
1. Purchase a few of their books or magazines to get a taste for their style. If you're contacting an agent, find out who they're representing so you can purchase some of their work.

2. Study their book. Tear apart the magazine. Absorb the style, tone, and rhythm.

3. Read and study their guidelines. You can save yourself a lot of time and trouble by sending publishers and agents appropriate material.

4. Write a killer query (if you're unsure how to do this, read the chapter called, "Power Queries" later in this book).

5. Then keep busy while you wait for their response.

Can I send the manuscript to other publishers while I'm waiting for a decision?
Absolutely. It's your manuscript and you may market it however you prefer.

However, please let your prospective publisher know if another publisher is considering your manuscript at the same time they're evaluating it. It's very frustrating for a publisher to spend their time reviewing a manuscript... to print and mail copies of it to their readers... then discuss it thoroughly... only to find out it's no longer available.

Let them know if you're presenting a simultaneous submission so they can decide whether they'd like to take the chance on reviewing a manuscript that may not be available.

What's the difference between a wholesaler and distributor and why should I know this?

A wholesaler (like Ingram and Baker & Taylor) carry your book in their catalog and make it available to book sellers.

A good distributor will help promote your book to book sellers and (sometimes) other markets.

You need a publisher who uses both a distributor and a wholesaler. If they don't, your book will not have much distribution. You also need a publisher who has a marketing plan outside the Internet. The Internet is a very good tool to sell books, but not all book sales occur online. Plus, the more outlets your book enjoys, the more streams of income it enjoys, the less your chance of getting stung when one particular market goes belly up and/or changes terms to make selling more difficult.

You need to be aware of this information so you know what you're up against. A publisher with only a wholesaler means you'll have fewer people on your "team" pitching your book. A distributor will help sell your book. This is wonderful because the more people actively promoting your book, the more sales you'll make.

Either way, however, plan on promoting your title a lot.

Does this mean I don't have to promote my book if a reputable publisher publishes it?

Absolutely not. You are (and always will be) your book's greatest promoter. Your publisher will do what they can to help promote your book... but realize they're promoting a list of titles. They're viewing a different picture than you:

You focus on your career, they're focusing on the overall health of their company.

You'll want to promote your book every way you can. There are tons of books on this subject. Create a website. Write articles for e-mags. Do everything you can to establish yourself as a quality writer, an authority in your field, and book sales will follow.

You'll need to work as a team with your publisher to make your book as profitable as possible.

If you're self publishing, promotion will become second nature. Do everything you can to get your book into Ingram and/or Baker and Taylor. Then start pitching to various distributors to get even more exposure for your title.

What is a galley?

A galley is a copy of your book that has a plain white cover. They're used for pre-publication reviews, publicity, and we use them to double-check for typos and errors. Some big time reviewers will not review a book once it's published. That's why the publicity period before your book actually comes off the press is so important.

You'll find a sample galley cover later in this book.

With the current glut of POD authors, I've seen very few publishers use galleys lately. That's too bad. We still send them to some of our beta readers. In fact, our commitment to these underutilized gems is so deep that we often print them in house.

If your prospective publisher doesn't send galleys, either in print or in an ebook format, seriously rethink working with them.

I've read that some publishing houses give their authors "author discounts" when they buy a bunch of books. Why would I want to purchase extra books?

It's always great when a publisher will allow their authors to purchase their books at a discount.

This is good for authors because… in a word… profits.

When your publishing company sells your book you'll receive (in a good case scenario) a 10 percent royalty. However, if you purchased 100 books, you'll often receive up to a 50 percent discount on the retail price. Any book you sell (like at a book signing, book fair, online (you have a website with a simple shopping cart... right?) would represent a profit of 50 percent instead of your usual 10 percent.

However, if your publisher demands that you purchase extra copies (often non-discounted) of your book as a part of your publishing agreement, decline to work with them. This means you're working with a vanity publisher who makes their profits on what you purchase, not on properly promoting and selling your books to legitimate readers.

Where should my readers be able to purchase my books?

Your readers should be able to purchase their books wherever they want to purchase them... not just online or at your publisher's website.

Find a bookstore-friendly publisher who deals with wholesalers and distributors so your local store won't have any trouble getting copies of your book.

What Questions Should I Ask Before I Sign With A Publisher?

Do you charge any fees?
If the answer is "yes" don't sign any contract.

How long will my book be in print?
If possible, you want to decide how long your book will be in print.

How long does a contract last?
Some contracts last "forever" while others have a sundown period when all rights will revert back to you. Obviously, you want to shoot for the latter, rather than the former.

I once met an author whose contract was so long-term that it mentioned sending royalties to her "grandchildren" and "great grandchildren." It went on to stipulate that even if the book went out of print, all rights stayed with the publishing company.

Yikes. That's not fair.

You want control of your work along with your career.

What rights do you require and for how long do you have them?

Don't sign over your rights longer than a couple years. Make sure all rights revert back to you when the contract expires. Also make note of how options like film rights, e-books, and audio books are handled.

Do I have to purchase books as a part of my publishing agreement?

The answer should be "no." Although you may want to purchase books (at a discount) for your own purposes, you shouldn't be required to purchase books.

What are publishers looking for when they read my query?

Whenever we receive a query, the first thing we look for is to see if the writer read our guidelines. If they didn't take time to read our guidelines, we question whether they really want to work with Filbert Publishing or are simply contacting a long line of potential publishers.

Next, we scan the letter to see if the project is appropriate for our company. If the manuscript is about anything except something in our niche, we stop reading and slip a rejection letter into the SASE.

If the author didn't include a SASE, we toss the letter in the recycling bin.

We also look for signs that the query was mass-mailed to other publishers as well. "Dear Editor" is a tip off because our guidelines clearly state that "Maury" is the person who receives these queries. If the e-mail/letter says "Dear Beth," I know that this person probably subscribes to Writing Etc. and I'll give this letter special attention since they're obviously a reader of the e-mag.

After we decide whether the writer's acquainted with Filbert Publishing, the next thing we look for is clear, concise writing. A well-written query often mirrors a well-written manuscript.

We watch for active verbs. We look for a compelling idea. We also keep an eye towards marketability.

Finally, the tone of the query is important. We're looking for upbeat writers with a smooth, confident, and enthusiastic writing style. A fearful, uncertain, and/or angry query will certainly result in a rejection letter.

You didn't have much good to say about the POD business model. Are there any circumstances when you'd recommend publishing a book as a POD title?

Absolutely. Please allow me to tell you a quick story:

I received two phone calls within a couple weeks. Two smart freelancers. Both nearly snared in the same writing scam.

It goes like this:

After months, if not years, of submitting their books to publishers and receiving scores of rejection letters, they finally received the "OK" to submit their latest work to what they thought were reputable publishers.

One small problem. Each had a niggling sensation in the pit of their stomach that simply wouldn't subside.

"We love the manuscript!" the publisher proclaimed. "Brilliant. It'll sell like gangbusters!"

Still, the nagging sensation persisted.

Then they e-mailed me complex e-mails detailing their situation.

"What's your phone number," I asked, "this is way to complicated to try to unravel via e-mail."

Onward they sent their phone numbers to me and I rang each of them.

As they spoke it became disappointingly clear that they were indeed caught up in a fairly common publishing situation.

I won't bore you with the minute details. However, on a broader scale I can say this:

When you are searching for a publisher of any sort, your mantra is, "Money flows towards the writer, not away from the writer."

Both these authors had found "publishers" who offered to "publish" their books for a fee. Really BIG fees.

This got me to thinking… if you're going to pay to publish your book, why not simply self publish? After all, publishers who claim to "publish" your book, then charge you setup fees, cover art fees, editing fees, annual hosting fees, and inflated book prices are not publishers.

Publishers are supposed to write checks, not collect fees.

If a "publisher" is "helping" you self publish your book, your best bet is to simply self publish it rather than get your name tangled with a company that may or may not have a reputable reputation.

I've heard of too many authors who are astounded to discover (after all the contracts were signed) that they hadn't found a publisher, but that the company was "assisting them in self publishing their book."

This clearly wasn't what they had hoped to find when their book got accepted by the company.

But most authors make the best of it and struggle against the stigma that many of these "Print on Demand" (POD) "publishers" have created for themselves, rightly or wrongly deserved.

Had most of these authors known that they were about to get caught between thinking they'd found a "publisher" and realizing the publisher viewed them as "self publishing" they would have simply opted for the second option and deleted the middle man.

This is what I advised these two writers to do.

If you're going to pay one cent to get published, hop ship

and self publish. With so many options available today, why not reap all the profits if you're going to have to work your tail off promoting your book?

You've got online publicity options available that are simple to use and dirt cheap to implement.

You've got a whole world of digital printing beckoning you to jump in and realize your dream.

Plus, you can totally eliminate the stigma of being affiliated with a POD publisher which means reviewers won't automatically reject your book. Bookstores could take a chance on stocking it (provided you supply bookstore friendly terms). Industry people won't wrinkle their noses at you.

You see, Print on Demand book printing is a fabulous technology. However, the Print on Demand business model that many POD publishers have developed, call for them to achieve the bulk of their profits not from book sales (because many of these books are anything but readable), but from author fees.

Now, I know, writer scams exist and will continue to thrive as long as authors are desperate to see their work in print. But to wallow in the negativity of it all won't suit either of us. It is what it is.

Especially when that same negative situation can shine the light on an incredible publishing opportunity open to every writer... self publishing using digital technology is powerful, wonderful, and one of the best developments since the printing press.

The resources are available. With the maturation of the Internet, promotion is darn near effortless.

And all this new technology will allow your writing to see the light of day.

Our future is truly bright. And there's something special about witnessing the birth of a new dream, a new publishing company. I know these fine writers will write the words they were born to write... and those words will make it onto the printed page.

I truly love my job and am absolutely grateful every time a dream takes flight.

Tell me what happens after a publisher accepts a manuscript for publication.

I can't speak for every publishing company, but here's how we handle the publishing process:

1.   The first thing we do is get the manuscript in an electronic format. Then we proof and edit it. Then comes laying out the book block. We (and most other publishers) need an electronic manuscript (usually in the Microsoft Word format (.doc) or Rich Text File (.rtf) to do this. Then after reviewing each page, it's off to the printer.

2.   Next, we assign an ISBN number to the manuscript. "ISBN" stands for "International Standard Book Number." It's a 13 digit number that uniquely identifies each book. Here's an example of an ISBN (Bookland EAN) bar code:

ISBN 978-1-932794-13-7

In checking out the ISBN:

The first three digits (978) comprise the EAN. The 978 means it's a book.

The "0" is the "Group" code... the country of origin.

The following six digits (932794) identify the publisher... that's us. :)

The next two digits (96) identify the title.

The final digit is a check number. It's complex math stuff.

The square bar code next to the ISBN identifies the price of the book.

3.   Next, we format the text and send an "e-galley" to the author for their approval. We also decide on a release date. Once the author approves the inside text format and date, we move onto the next step.

4.   Now we create a cover for the galley. It's a plain white

cover, minimal color, just gives specifics about your book.

5.   Now we write a press release promoting your book. Here's an example:

FROM: Filbert Publishing
140 NE 3rd Street
Box 326
Kandiyohi, MN 56251
CONTACT: Beth Ann Erickson
Phone 320-382-6662
FilbertPublishing@FilbertPublishing.com

For Immediate Release

New book reveals how freelance writers can jumpstart their writing career and snag paying assignments.

Kandiyohi, MN. While many writers struggle to survive in today's sluggish economy, some are doing better than ever… largely because they have mastered the proven but little practiced strategy known as "Effective Self Promotion."

That's the opinion of Beth Ann Erickson, a freelance writer, editor of Writing Etc., the free e-mag for writers (http://FilbertPublishing.com) and author of the newly published book, "Jumpstart Your Writing Career and Snag Paying Assignments."

"Many freelance writers never see their finances thrive. Although the economy may be rough, it is possible to make a nice living doing what we love. All you need is a simple marketing plan and you can watch your freelance career bloom."

Here's a short excerpt from Erickson's book detailing ten strategies you can use today to land business and make a great living as a writer:

First, approach your local newspaper editor and ask if they need someone to cover meetings. If they do, you're on your way to building a huge clip file. Not only that, but you've just taken the first step to building a solid writing career.

Armed with your local clips, you can start approaching bigger markets. Markets like small and mid-sized magazines that are hungry for new articles. Start querying them and wait for their response. (Technique 2.)

While you're waiting to hear from your magazine queries, chat with a few of the mayors, city council people, school board members, etc. that you've met at your meetings. Most of them are business people.

Ask if they need their brochures updated, ads or direct mail letters written, or if they need a writer-for-hire for any project they may have brewing. You'd be surprised how many business people will take you up on your offer after they've witnessed your diligence and accuracy while covering their meetings. (Technique 3.)

To start attracting more commercial clients, you can run a small ad in your local paper. As your expertise increases, place more ads in surrounding papers. Maybe you'll want to write a snappy classified ad in the business section. (Technique 4.)

Join your local Chamber of Commerce. You'll meet business owners and make invaluable contacts. (Technique 5.)

Another technique to keep the money rolling in as a freelance writer is to have lots of irons in the fire. Along with the magazine queries, and copywriting, always have a book in the works and send out proposals for it.

I know one local writer who has cultivated a devoted clientèle who has her write all their correspondence… including Christmas letters. Your projects are only limited by your imagination. (Technique 6.)

Make goals each day. Decide how many queries you'll send out. Decide how many sales letters you'll mail. How many words are you going to write in your book? How many new contacts are you going to make this week? Make your goals… then follow through with them. (Technique 7.)

Ask and you may receive. Don't be afraid to ask for what you want. If you're a stringer for your local newspaper, ask the editor if it's possible for them to run a small ad promoting your business at a discount (after all you're a staff writer.) If you run an e-mag, ask to exchange links or ads. If you write for local businesses, ask them to recommend your writing services to their friends. (Technique 8.)

Never tell anyone your phone number. GIVE it to them. Print up a bunch of business cards and whenever anyone asks for your phone number, give them your card instead. (Technique 9.)

Carry your latest project with you. If you've written a book, take it wherever you go. If you just finished a big copywriting project, have it nearby. Got an article in the latest issue of a magazine or newspaper? Better bring it with you.... Nothing sparks a conversation faster than "What 'cha been up to lately?" Then, next thing you know, you've got a prospective customer. (Technique 10.)

Finally, perfect your craft, become the best writer you can be, promote your business, and you'll soon have more work than you can handle.

To receive a copy of "Jumpstart Your Writing Career and Snag Paying Assignments," send 15.95 (plus 3.50 Priority Mail Shipping) to: Filbert Publishing, Box 326, Kandiyohi, MN 56251-0326. Credit card orders are accepted at http://FilbertPublishing.com/

Beth Ann Erickson is a freelance writer, copywriter, and publisher based in Kandiyohi, MN. She's had hundreds of articles published throughout the US and Canada. She's the author of The Almach (a novel), and the nonfiction title, "Jumpstart Your Writing Career and Snag Paying Assignments." You can subscribe to Writing Etc., the free e-mag that will make your writing sparkle, help you write killer articles, and get you on to the road to publication – fast, by surfing to http://FilbertPublishing.com.

-30-

Jumpstart Your Writing Career and Snag Paying Assignments by Beth Ann Erickson. Published by Filbert

Publishing. Second Edition 5 X 8 trade paperback, 200 pages.   ISBN   1-932794-14-X. $15.95.   Publication, September, 2006.

(Editor's Note: The -30- at the end of a press release signals the end of it.)

6.   Next we get a Library of Congress number. Many publishers, especially POD houses, skip this step. However, if you want your title considered for library placement, you'll have to get an LOC number.

7.   Now we send a minimum of 5 printed galleys to our author to distribute to their contacts.

8.   The same day we send galleys to our pre-selected list of reviewers... places like Kirkus, Publisher's Weekly, Quality Books, etc. (It never hurts to shoot for the big guys...)

9.   Now we can breathe a while... but not long. Next we create the book's cover. This is a crucial step because without a great cover, your book is doomed. We work closely with our designer and author to come up with a design that both are thrilled with.

10.   Now we register the ISBN number with RRBowker. Your book is now set to go to our distributors, Baker and Taylor and/or Ingram.

11.   We (and our authors) are busy contacting reviewers both online and offline at this point.

12.   We also send review copies to appropriate book clubs.

13.   We add the title to the Filbert Publishing catalog.

14.   Now, we research other promotional opportunities that may not be mainstream, but are well within our niche. These often prove to be very lucrative.

15.   We create book descriptions we'll need for our promotional mailings.

16.   Finally, we release the book... and always keep our eyes open for new promotional opportunities.

Tell me about writing contests. How can I know if a contest is a scam?

Unfortunately, many "scam" contests are found in the back of writing magazines. They also thrive online. You'd think someone would filter scam artists out of their magazine, but they don't.

But you can be prepared... here's how contest scams work:

Once you answer the ad, you send in a hefty "entrance" fee. Immediately, you receive a letter saying you've "WON!" After they stroke your ego for a while, they hit you up for more money to purchase an extremely expensive book that will house your poem/short story/whatever. They also ask you to purchase books for all your relatives, neighbors, and friends.

Problem is, everybody's a winner with these guys and your quality poem/story/whatever will probably sit next to some sort of awful rendition of "Roses are red..." or "It was a dark and stormy night...."

Here are some general tips to help you avoid getting scammed in a writing or poetry contest:

Don't pay more than $10 to $15 to join. A small administrative fee is just fine... but to charge $50 to $100 bucks to join a contest is extreme. (I know... Writer's Digest charges mucho bucks for their contests... but they're Writer's Digest. They're legit and can charge what they'd like.)

Find out whether your prize includes a book in which your story/poem will appear. If it doesn't, then ask how much the book costs. If it's a hefty fee, you're probably on the verge of being scammed.

If you decide to enter the contest, you've won, and you'll receive a free book, don't send more money to include your bio or picture. A legitimate company will include these extras at no charge.

Don't attend any "presentation ceremonies" unless you get to attend for free. Some companies charge their "winners" up to $1,000 to receive their "award of excellence." Crazy but true... desperate writers fall for this scam every year.

As with most of the anti-scam advice in this book, if you remember that money is supposed to flow towards the writer, not away from them, you can avoid most "contest" scams as well.

Can You Give Me some Resources To Make This Process Easier?

Absolutely! There are some fabulous on and off-line resources available to you. Let's start with markets... if you need to find places to send your writing, here's where to start:

Writer's Market Online: http://WritersMarket.com
Writing Etc.: http://FilbertPublishing.com
Writer's Weekly: http://WritersWeekly.com
Writing for Dollars: http://WritingForDollars.com

If you want free writing tips and guidance, here are a few websites you'll want to visit:

Writing Etc.: http://FilbertPublishing.com
Absolute Write: http://absolutewrite.com
National Association of Women Writers: http://NAWW.org

Writer's Warnings and Scam Alert sites:
Predators and Editors:
http://anotherealm.com/prededitors/peba.htm
Google Groups: http://google.com

Helpful Books:
Anything by Robert W. Bly. He's a master when it comes to this topic.

Writing Books:
On Writing by Stephen King
Lessons From a Lifetime of Writing by David Morrell

Writing Career:

Jumpstart Your Writing Career and Snag Paying Assignments by Beth Ann Erickson

101 No Cost (And No Cost) Techniques to Turbo Charge Your Freelance Income by Beth Ann Erickson

Guerilla Marketing for Writers by Jay Levenson

OK. What's a query and how do I write an effective one?

We've included a copy of Beth's wildly popular e-book called "Power Queries" in a later chapter. Read it, follow the instructions, and you'll write an awesome query.

Isn't this book a long advertisement for Filbert Publishing?

Nope. We have more manuscripts and more potential authors contacting us than we could hope to publish. We wrote this as a manual for writers... there are far too many horror stories floating into the Filbert Publishing offices. I figured we better write something to help counteract all the scams popping up.

Writers need to be informed. Learn how to spot red flags and know when to leave what you once thought was a great opportunity.

You've worked very hard on your manuscript. Give it the treatment it deserves by not settling for less than what your hard work merits.

If you see any of these red flags in a publishing house you're considering, run... don't walk... away from them.

Paying for publishing:

Any time a publisher, agent, or editor asks you for money, politely decline. These people are (in all likelihood) scam artists who prey on writer's dreams. Legit publishers will not ask you to pony up dough for any reason.

Purchasing books as a part of your publishing agreement:

If you have to buy a set number of books and sell them

yourself, this isn't a legitimate publishing company.

Paying for edits:
If a publishing house or agent "just happens" to be affiliated with an editing company that will edit your manuscript for a fee, decline to work with them. Legit publishers and agents will edit your manuscript free of charge.

Setup Fees:
Unless you specifically want to self-publish your manuscript, there's no reason to pay setup fees... ever. A legitimate publisher does not charge "setup fees."

Reading Fees:
A literary agent I once contacted wrote this: "With the inundation of quality manuscripts, I feel I must charge you for my time to review yours." Bull-doggie. Forget it. Any publisher or agent who charges a reading fee is a scam artist and isn't worth your time.

Contract Woes:
Finding a good contract can be tough. But if you know a few contract-pitfalls, you'll make a much more educated decision as to whether you want to sign it. You'd also be wise to contact an attorney to thoroughly read any potential contract, too.
Here are a few clauses you'll want to avoid:
Purchasing Manuscript outright – you don't want to sell your manuscript. If you do this, you forfeit all royalties forever.
E-book Rights – make sure you don't sign over all your e-book rights. E-books are an interesting turn in the publishing world, but without utilizing certain strategies, they can be a tough sell. Most traditional publishers mess up their ebook sales in a big ugly way. However, some savvy self publishers find them exceedingly profitable. If you're pondering a

publishing contract, make sure you get at least a 40 to 50 percent royalty when your publisher decides to make your book available as an e-book. If they only want print rights, publish the ebook yourself. It's worth it.

Length of contract – don't go more than a couple years on a contract. A long term contract can feel r-e-a-l-l-y long if you're attached to a publisher who you're having a personality conflict with or who you think is sub-standard.

Rights – It's just fine to assign your rights to a publisher for a short period of time. Don't assign them world-wide rights. English speaking… OK. But try to retain as many rights as possible.

Royalty schedule – it's ideal to have your royalties based on the retail price of your book instead of "net receipts" or "net profits." Here's the difference. Suppose your book retails for $12.95. If you're earning a 10 percent royalty, your take on the title will be $1.30. No matter what happens, you'll always receive $1.30 for every book that sells if your royalty is based on the retail price.

If your royalty is based on "net receipts," your royalty will be less. Let's pretend that most of your sales came through the bookstore system. Baker and Taylor (the wholesaler who supplies bookstores), demand a 55 percent discount on most of the books they carry. So your 12.95 book now "nets" the publisher only $5.83. If your royalty is based on "net receipts" your ten percent is now a mere .58 per book sold.

It gets worse. If your royalty is based on "net profits" your publisher can take your $12.95 book, subtract 55 percent for Baker and Taylor (leaving $5.83), subtract the postage to get it to Baker and Taylor, subtract any costs for promotion, heating and air conditioning… whatever. Your grand profit of .58 per book can be reduced to pennies by the time the term "profit" is defined.

If you must sign a "net" contract (common for ebooks), make sure the "net" is spelled out. In an ebook situation, the "net" is often retail price minus bookstore fees.

"We can change this contract at any time." Here's an

actual clause in a contract I once signed:

"Changes to this agreement may be posted without notice to the Author. THE AUTHOR'S CONTINUED PARTICIPATION IN OUR PROGRAMS AFTER THE COMPANY'S POSTING OF ANY CHANGES WILL CONSTITUTE THE AUTHOR'S ACCEPTANCE OF SUCH CHANGES OR MODIFICATIONS. IF THE AUTHOR DOES NOT AGREE TO ANY CHANGES TO THIS AGREEMENT, THE AUTHOR MUST TERMINATE THIS AGREEMENT."

Talk about getting the short end of the stick, eh? They can make changes at any time, without notice, and my continued participation in their company is my implied consent. It's a bummer of a phrase that stung my pocketbook towards the end of our affiliation as publisher and author.

You want a contract that says that any changes to the contract must be agreed to by both parties in writing. That way you're protected if your publisher suddenly decides to change the way they're publishing your book.

Carefully examine any contract you're offered for any of these red flags.

No Promotion from Publisher

If your publisher doesn't promote their titles, they're an "author mill" who makes the majority of their money selling books to their authors and their surrounding communities, friends, and neighbors. Good publishers promote their titles.

Paying for Promotion

Unless you're self publishing, do not pay for any "promotional packages." A reputable publisher will promote your title as part of their daily business operations.

No Galleys sent to reviewers

A good review in a widely-read magazine (or e-magazine) will sell more books than you can imagine. The hitch is that many reviewers want to read prepublication galleys. If your publisher doesn't manufacture galleys and/or make egalleys freely available, it's unlikely that you'll sell many books.

No input on cover/text layout

I'm getting picky here. But when my first book came out, I absolutely hated the cover. I'd have given my eyeteeth to have a book that made me proud.

If you're working with a small publishing house, it's only common courtesy that they'll give you final say on the cover design. After all, you're the ultimate owner of that book and with any luck, it'll follow you for a very long time.

Step Three: Start Contacting Publishing Houses and Continue Mastering Your Craft.

The following pages contain some sections you don't want to miss. Absorb the information and you'll cut your learning curve by a lot. Probably years.

First up, you'll discover how to write incredible queries. Craft your query following these guidelines and you'll increase your chances of hitting paydirt on every manuscript you write.

Next, you'll find Ten Steps to Freelancing Freedom. This chapter outlines ten easy steps you can follow to ignite your writing income and keep a steady stream of work coming your way.

Then you can peruse a chapter called, Beyond the Writer's Market... Finding Lucrative Writing Assignments in Any Economy.

After that, you can dig through a simple self publishing primer called, How to Write, Produce, and Sell Profitable Books.

Finally, we've included an issue of my own e-mag, Writing Etc. so you can get a feel for what an online ezine is like. These little electronic wonders can really kick-start your writing income.

Lastly, you can check out a typical author-friendly publishing contract. Acquaint yourself with it so when you get presented with a contract of your own, you'll know what to look for.

Oh... and be sure to check out the final chapter of this book....

Power Queries
How to write a convincing letter selling almost anything...

You're sitting at your desk, wracking your brain, staring at the blank computer screen. A hole forms in your stomach as you struggle to form words to begin that accursed letter. That accursed query.

You've got an article idea but don't know how to get that letter written so you can sell it to an editor.

Well, here are some techniques that will make writing that next query a breeze:

The first sentence of your letter is the most important. By reading your opening, your prospective editor decides whether your query is something of interest or worthless junk. Your first sentence must somehow capture your reader's attention and entice him to read on. Here are a few ideas to help you ...

Start Your Query With Style

Jump straight into your story. Cut and paste the first couple sentences of your article directly into your query. Here's an example:

"Mary Olson thought she was sending her child to a safe preschool that morning, but by late afternoon she would find out her perceptions were completely wrong...."

Is your curiosity piqued? Would this example keep you reading? If you're interested, chances are an editor would be.

Make an announcement.

"For the first time in 20 years, the only eyewitness to the [insert disaster here] tells his story."

This approach is effective if your editor wants, needs, or thinks your article idea will interest his audience. If you use this approach make sure you've targeted your magazine sufficiently and captured their voice.

Tell a story.

Queries written in a story format have great reader appeal. Everybody loves a good story and usually wants to find out how it ends so they keep reading. How many times have you stopped what you were doing because you didn't want to miss the end of Paul Harvey's "The Rest of the Story?" So shorten your article enough to include a good chunk of it in your query. Perhaps it could begin something like this:

Twenty-five years ago, a man did the impossible. In a harsh economy, he defied the experts, he ignored his accountants, and followed his dream. In the middle of an economically distressed area, he opened a store that sold only men's suits....

This opener went on to tell a rather intriguing story that drew me through the opening, the body, all the way to the close. It was a good query....

Begin your query with a provocative quote.

It should contain news, a startling statistic or fact. It should be like the lead of a news story and make the reader want to read more. An example:

"Hold it carefully and take a deep breath; this little book may well represent the future of literary magazines...."

Or how about this quote?

"Did you know that 75 percent of American homes have a silent killer in their basement?"

These quotes are strong – and intriguing to boot! I don't know many editors who wouldn't want to know a little more about these article ideas.

Ask a question – but make sure your question is interesting or important to the reader. Your question should arouse the reader's curiosity. And here are some examples:

What's your definition of "fun?"

What isn't the corporate-owned media telling you?

How much do you love your job?

A word of caution here: Be absolutely sure your question

is provocative enough to arouse attention or it will fall flat. Try to use open-ended questions. Use yes/no questions carefully. If your reader answers the question and isn't intrigued, they may skip the rest of your letter. However, a well-phrased question will naturally draw your reader into the body of your letter.

Stress a benefit. A straightforward presentation of a strong benefit can out pull any other technique to get your letter started. Here's an example from a newsletter query:

"READ THIS OR DIE. Today you have a 95 percent chance of eventually dying from a disease or condition for which there is already a known cure somewhere on the planet."

I know… this one's bordering on hyperbole but you have to admit… it does attract your attention. It would definitely work if you wrote a strong letter after this first sentence….

Write a good anecdote. An anecdote will pull your editor into your story and showcase your writing capabilities.

Quotes and dialogue add color to your query. Beginning your letter with a conversation or quote will make it stand out.

DON'T OPEN WITH dumb jokes, puns, technical jargon, and unsubstantiated claims. Keep your letter brief, to the point, and with an eye towards your potential editor's needs.

Finally, from the first word you write, until the last word of your P.S., ALWAYS remember to write peer to peer. Write using the language of your reader so your editor knows you'll be able to capture the voice of his publication.

Every magazine has a "voice." The language used by a publication like the New Yorker is very different than the words used by a magazine like Maximum PC/Minimum BS. READ a few issues of the publication you want to write for. Then write using their distinct "voice."

When you match your voice to the voice of your reader you're saying, "Look, I'm like you. I know your problem, I've been through it myself, and I've found a solution." Here's an example:

"One day years ago my writing professor handed back a story I had written, shook her head gravely, and said, "This is so bad it makes me want to quit teaching."

Writing peer to peer – writing as you would to a friend – is the tone you want to cultivate in every query you write. Imagine you're writing a personal letter or an e-mail and use that language. Attempting to impress your reader with your grasp of the American Language will only succeed in alienating them – and in most of your queries being rejected.

OK. You've started your letter. Let's assume your editor is intrigued enough to read on. This leads me to the next section of your sales letter: You need to write…

The Lead
Your lead is the section of your letter between your first sentence and the body. Your lead needs to be vivid, short, use ultra specific words, and compel the reader to read further.

You can use a newspaper-type lead that answers the questions: When, Where, What, Who, Why, and How.

You can also use an inverted pyramid structure where you lead with the most important information and save the details for later. When you use this structure you generally arouse interest in the beginning of your letter, provide specifics in the following paragraphs, then close with your key point. After your lead is complete, you can move on to the body of your letter.

By using ultra-specific words, your lead vibrates with life. Instead of car, use Buick. Instead of dog, say Rat Terrier. Scour each sentence you write and look for words you can make even more specific.

The Immaculate Body
The "body" of your letter contains your sales pitch. And yes… queries are very similar to sales letters because you are, in fact, trying to sell your article to an editor. So your body contains your sales pitch. But don't worry. You won't have to write a long and detailed body because queries

shouldn't be longer than two pages unless you absolutely have to make it longer.

The body of your letter tells specifically what you want your reader to do – whether it's to purchase your article, contact you for more information, or read your article on spec. Here are a few tips to make your query more effective:

Organize your most powerful selling points. Write each point you want to cover on a note card and put them in the order you'll write about them. As you write each point on your note card, emphasize how it will benefit the reader. Also, think about how you'll transition from one point to the next to make sure that your letter will flow smoothly.

Write with your prospective editor in mind – not you. How will your editor's readers benefit from your article? Will they understand what you're saying? Are you telling them anything useful? If you were reading this, would you be persuaded to buy your article?

One way to build your reader's interest and "hook" him is to use the word "you" in your copy. Read any magazine on the market and you'll find that 90 percent of the ads contain the word "you." Use of the word "you" will answer your reader's question: "What's in this for me? How does this affect me? Why should I spend time reading this?" Notice the difference:

Me-Oriented writing:
When I first became a writer, I hoped I could change my world and make it a little better. That's why I wrote, "Power Queries." Power Queries will help me achieve that goal because it will help other writers get published.

You-Oriented Copy:
I'm sure that you're a lot like many of the writers I meet every day. Like them, I'd bet you hoped you'd make a difference in your world. That's why I wrote Power Queries. It will help you structure your letter from start to finish... and will get you on the road to publication – fast. (Italics added

for emphasis.)

Use interesting facts and figures when you need to. Quote your sources. This establishes credibility and helps the editor realize you know your stuff.

Let the editor know if you have a sidebar to go with the piece. Also mention any relevant photographs you may be able to include along with graphs and graphics that would complement the article.

Explain how your piece is relevant to the reader.

Divide your copy into short paragraphs. There's nothing more intimidating than long blocks of solid text. Break up your body. Use short paragraphs.

Write in crisp, short, snappy sentences. Because we don't always speak in complete sentences, don't be too afraid to write like you speak. That means you can often get away with ending your sentences with prepositions. Sometimes you'll even use sentence fragments.

Always remember your goal IS NOT to write the perfect sentence – your goal is to sell your article. Period. (However, vary your length of your sentences to make your writing flow.)

Use simple words and avoid jargon. When you're writing a query, you're trying to communicate with your reader, not impress them with your huge vocabulary or boost your ego. Always remember you're trying to SELL – not impress.

Write in a conversational style. How would you phrase your sales pitch if you were speaking to your reader in person? Write like you speak and you'll hold on to your reader.

Be credible. You can establish credibility by knowing what you're writing about. This may include providing credentials that make you the best source to provide the article. Mention your education, life experience, publishing credits, and hobbies if they're relevant to the topic. You'll also want to include a short biography to introduce yourself.

Include a word count of your article.

Get the editor's name right. Subscribe to Writers Market Online or Write Market Reports so you know exactly who you're sending the letter to.

Don't use weasel phrases like "I think that…" "The article may…" and "I'll do my best to explain…" You wrote the article. You better know your information. When you write your query, sound like you know what you're talking about. Use phrases like, "The article will…" and "I know…."

Check all your facts one more time to make sure they're correct.

KEEP IT SHORT. No more than two pages

Always send a Self Addressed Stamped Envelope (or SASE for short.)

Know what the publisher needs, then give it to them. Don't send them inappropriate materials or the types of stories they don't print.

Closing the Deal

In your closing paragraph you need to clearly state the action you want your reader to take. Here's a nice "call to action.":

"I look forward to hearing from you." "Let me know what you think. I've enclosed a SASE for your convenience."

Make it short, to-the-point and very clear.

Make it easy for your editor to respond by including a Self Addressed Stamped Envelope (or SASE for short.) If you don't include a SASE, in all likelihood you WILL NOT be contacted by the publication you just queried. Plus you'll look like a rank amateur.

The Letter's Done!

That about covers it! All you have to do is sign your name and add a P.S. if you have something irresistible to add to your query.

P.S. I've just been commissioned to do an article on XXX for the XXX issue of XXXX Magazine. Be sure to watch for it!

Most readers skim your headline, then head straight to the P.S. So if you include a P.S., make it strong. Make it reinforce your credibility.

Now you need to proofread, proofread, and proofread. Look for typos. Look for unneeded words. Are your sentences concise or wordy?

Print the letter on nice white medium bond paper using a quality printer. And never mail your only copy. DO NOT send hand written queries. DO NOT send queries on pretty paper scented with perfume. Remember, queries are business letters and should look like them.

Now all you have to do is send the letter to your prospective editor. While you're waiting for a response, draft a few more queries for other articles and send them to other editors. It's helpful to have a number of irons in the fire so you are never caught with nothing to work on.

Fire up your computer and work on a novel or two. Draft a sales letter and try to draw some corporate writing your way. Become a writer for hire and write for people in your community. Get going writing a nonfiction book.

You're a writer. You may as well earn a few bucks while you're working on something you enjoy! The possibilities are endless.

I hope these tips help you write a stronger query that will attract tons of writing assignments. And if you're looking for more guidance on how to make a living as a writer be sure to check out FilbertPublishing.com.

Ten Steps to Freelancing Freedom: How to Create the Freelance Career of Your Dreams An Extended Transcript of the CD Available at FilbertPublishing.com

In my opinion, working as a freelance writer is by far the best profession in the world.

What other job allows you to read in your spare time, hang out with interesting people, invest in all the solitude you want, and surf the web 'till your heart's content?

PLUS... if you do it correctly, you can get paid for all these activities.

I think the reason I enjoy my freelance career is because it's not so much a "career" as much as it's a lifestyle. When you decide to jump into the freelancing pool, I have a hunch you'll find yourself living your profession as much as working in it as well.

For example, who knows when a great writing idea will crash into your consciousness?

Whether you're at the beach, sitting at your desk, or waiting in the vet's office, you'll have to be prepared to grab onto every good idea that graces your presence and hang on tight. This means you carry a little pad of paper with you. This means you keep yourself in the mindset of writing. This means you don't ever have any real "time off."

But on the other hand, you have the freedom to raise your family... spend your time as you wish... write whenever and wherever you want... and make a nice living doing this.

If this lifestyle interests you... if you want to make a living doing what you love to do... here are ten steps you can follow that can create the writing lifestyle of your dreams.

Step One: Set Up Your Work Space

First and foremost, your writing area should be comfortable. Whether you work in an office or carve out a writing niche in your bedroom... make sure it's a place where you want to spend a lot of time.

When I first started freelancing I worked out of a room in my basement. I thought I'd go crazy. The tiny window barely let in any light. On nice days, I felt like I was missing out on knowing what was going on outside. On rainy days I felt like I was missing all the excitement of a great storm outside. Every now and then I'd see a pair of legs walk by... that's how I knew someone was coming to visit.

Drove me nuts.

It didn't take me long to take over the entire front room of our rambler-type house. Today I have a large window in front of my desk. The huge picture window is directly to my right. Lucy (my Rat Terrier Wonder Dog and writing companion) lays on her table in front of the window.

Best of all, I don't feel like I'm missing out on anything. If Lucy goes ballistic, I just turn in my chair to see what she's barking at. I watch kids come home from school. The seasons change before my eyes. Best of all... I get to watch those wild summer thunderstorms form, rage, and dissipate... all from the comfort of my office.

Secondly, be sure you have enough space for your office.

Writing on your kitchen table is OK, but be aware that you'll need more room than you think. In fact, a dedicated work space is ideal.

As you grow your freelance business, you'll need plenty of room for reference books, reading materials, and magazines. You'll also want to invest in a computer and printer. You'll also want access to the Internet (if you don't already have this).

The 'net is a gold mine for freelance opportunities. It's also a great place to find reference materials for your articles. Beware, though... make sure your reference site is reputable or you may be using faulty information in your articles. As a freelancer, it's imperative that you always protect your reputation by using the best resource materials possible.

But I digress... let's get back to your work environment.

Third, you'll need a couple of file cabinets. One will organize your article research. Once you research an article, keep your materials and recycle as much as possible. For example, if you write an article for Dog Fancy called, "How to Train Rat Terriers," you can use the same sources and write a new article for Family Circle called, "How I got my Rat Terrier to Behave."

This file will also hold all the correspondence you'll accumulate as you make your way through your freelance profession. Keep copies of your queries here. Keep your rejection letters and acceptance ones as well. Poke copies of magazines you plan on contacting in here along with any other miscellaneous communications that you'll undoubtedly receive.

The other file cabinet will be your "swipe file." This cabinet will house junk mail.

Junk mail!?

Yup. You read correctly.

If you want to make a good living as a freelancer, you'll need to learn to write for businesses. Start locally by keeping every piece of advertising you receive from local businesses. Study it. Figure out ways to make it better. Then contact that company and offer to write their next mailing.

Beginning copywriters (writers who write for businesses) don't have any trouble earning at least $40 per hour. It's a great addition to your freelance income and a wonderful way to finance other writing projects.

Check the resource section at the back of this chapter for more information on learning how to write effective ad copy.

Finally... when you're deciding where to house your office, keep in mind you may want to have a place where you can "spread out." For example, when I'm in the middle of an assignment, I often have papers spread across the floor behind me... often five to eight feet worth. Whenever I need to check out a reference, I spin in my chair, grab the right sheet, and get right back to work.

I need a lot of space. Maybe you're the same as me... maybe you're not. But think about this before you choose where you'll write.

Also, I like loud music playing when I write. I have a friend who demands perfect silence. I like having Lucy near by. My friend goes crazy if anybody's in the room with her.

Think about all these factors when you're deciding on where you'll place your work area....

Step Two: Draft a Loose Business Plan

I admit it. I hate planning. That's why I made my business plan loose. Make yours as detailed as you'd like. Here are a few things you should include:

What will you call your writing business?

Many freelancers just call themselves something like, "Beth Ann Erickson... Freelance Writer."

Some get more specific. "Beth Ann Erickson, Marketing Expert and Freelance Advertising Copywriter"

Or, how 'bout this? "Beth Ann Erickson, Freelance Advertising Copywriter and Consultant"

Some people (like me) use a business name. I'm known as "Filbert Publishing and Writing"

The name you choose is totally up to you. Using your own name is an easy option because when you choose a name other than your own, you'll have to fill out a number of legal forms explaining that you're "doing business as" another name.

When I began Filbert Publishing, I had a quick chat with my accountant to find out what I needed to do to make myself legal. I'd suggest you do the same thing.

Next, you'll need to decide what you'll write.

Do you want to specialize in article writing? Copywriting? Fiction? Nonfiction? Perhaps you're an aspiring poet.

I'd suggest that you diversify as much as possible to keep as many income streams as possible flowing into the business.

Some writers dabble in mail order by creating products and sending full fledged direct mail packages to thousands of potential customers. Others sell products over the Internet.

The sky's the limit.

That's why it's a good idea to take a moment to decide what you LIKE to write, what kind of writing can create the income you desire, and then decide what the majority of your time will be spent on.

Now that you know what you enjoy writing, decide who your customers will be. Make a list. Crack open the Yellow pages... get your hands on a current Writer's Market... and get to work.

Next, you need to research fees. I mentioned earlier that beginning copywriters earn around $40 per hour. Read the Writer's Market and find out what publications are paying for articles. Target the higher paying markets but realize you'll probably have to sell a few articles for less money so you can build your clip file.

You can also contact local publications to find out what they pay their freelancers. If you get hooked up with a regular freelancing gig with a local newspaper, for example, you'll eventually get more clips than you'll know what to do with and receive invaluable experience in the world of freelancing.

Decide where you'll work. If you can't find a dedicated work space at home, perhaps you'll have to find a small office. Also realize you'll have more expenses if you move away from home. I've freelanced eight years out of my home and wouldn't want it any other way... but some people do. So decide where you want to spend your writing time.

Decide whether you'll have office hours. Will you accept business calls at 9:00 pm? Will you work weekends? What if you get a writing assignment with a tight deadline at 4:59 Friday? Perhaps you'll work with a flexible schedule... or maybe you want to be a 9 to 5er.

Choice is yours.

You also have to decide where the money will come from to finance this new business. Although freelance writing is a fairly low-expense business, you'll discover that it does require some cash flow.

You'll need to purchase paper, toner/ink, pens, pencils,

three-hole punch, stapler, paper for brochures, reference materials, books, magazines, Internet access, file cabinets, insurance... just to mention a few expenses.

Before you begin writing for clients, make a complete list of everything you can possibly need to begin your business. Separate that list into sections labeled, "Supplies I need ASAP," "Supplies I need later," "My wish list."

Let this list "rest" a while, add to it, subtract from it, and reorganize it, then go back to it one last time before you head out to the office supply store.

Step Three: Educate Yourself

Here's where you can really get the edge in your freelance writing career.

Take a look at any profession. Teachers must continue to earn Continuing Education Units to keep their license current. Sheet Metal Workers take classes on a regular basis to keep up to date with new government guidelines. (I know this because my husband is a sheet metal worker. □)

Freelancers who don't continue their education will become shallow, ineffective writers.

We need to be curious. We need a zest for life. We need to wonder why something is the way it is.

If you're going to be a life-long freelancer, you must be a life-long learner.

Take classes. Not just writing classes... take FUN classes. I once took an Abnormal Psych class because it sounded interesting. I used the knowledge from that class when I wrote Heart Songs, my second novel.

Purchase and read books. I'm a reference book junkie. I haunt flea markets, book stores, and thrift joints...and never walk out empty handed. Read everything and anything. You never know when an awesome idea will flit on your shoulder. Fiction, nonfiction, how-to... doesn't matter. Read. A lot.

Subscribe to magazines. Writer's Digest. Home and Garden. Maximum PC. People. Mad. Doesn't matter. Whatever interests you... read about it.

Subscribe to e-magazines. Most are free. E-mags will keep your finger on the pulse of what's new and hot. Paper mags often have a long waiting period between when they accept an article and when it runs. E-mags tend to be cutting edge with the newest information possible. Read e-mags to get a sense of what the paper mags will be running in a few months.

Now, I know you're a writer. So, why do I suggest that you read so much?

Simple. Stephen King in his book, "On Writing" explains it best: If you don't have time to read, you don't have the time or the tools to write.

The best writers are voracious readers. If you want to be the best writer you can be, read.

Step 4: Study Your Competition

You need to know who your competition is, whether you're writing articles, ad copy, or books. After you identify your competition, you need to study their style. Find out what they're doing right, and identify areas where you're better.

If you're writing ad copy, find out who they work for and why they were hired. Find out what their weaknesses are and fill that gap.

For example, if a local ad agency writes newspaper ads with fab graphics, but their copy is weak, offer to help them with that particular need.

If a magazine has great how-to writing articles, you can suggest that they hire you to write articles on how to market those wonderfully-written pieces.

When you know who your competition is and what they're doing, you can better create a strong plan of action that has a better than average chance of yielding results.

Step 5: Target the Markets You Want To Write For

What interests you? I'd never write for the high-tech road building industry. The subject doesn't interest me and I don't think it ever will.

However, throw a subject my way that holds my attention and I can come up with a great article/sales piece about it.

List your interests... then find out who needs this type of writing.

Decide if you want to specialize in a narrow subject or whether you'd rather be known as a "generalist."

A niche writer is someone who becomes an expert in a narrow subject. Robert W. Bly is a copywriter who writes about writing copy. He writes for a very narrow market. He's a renowned expert and makes a very good living.

A generalist is someone who writes on any subject. These writers write about everything from dogs to sewing machines... from weather to child rearing. It's pretty tough to find an expert "generalist" because these people usually aren't renown. However, you can make a very nice living as a generalist.

Step 6: Study Your Target Market

When you know who you want to write for, you need to study their format, their preferences, their style. Read the publication. Get on their mailing list. If you're a copywriter, pinpoint the weakness in their current promotional efforts. If you can strengthen that weakness, you're one step closer to landing the job.

When you're first starting out, write some articles on spec. Do the same thing with ads and other promo efforts. Mail them to a specific person in that company and see if they're interested in using it.

Always send your correspondence to an actual person. For example, if you send your query to "Filbert Publishing," chances are the wrong person will open it. It'll get stuck in a box, sit there for a few days, and perhaps after a couple weeks, it'll wind up on another desk. The correct person may (or may not) eventually get it... but it'll take a while.

On the other hand, if you read the Filbert Publishing guidelines... and perhaps scan a few past issues of Writing Etc., you'd know you need to send the query to Maury

Erickson. He'll receive it, open it, and give it his immediate attention.

Also, when we receive a query that starts with the words, "To Whom It May Concern," we'll know they haven't done their research. We'll read the query, but I'll admit we don't read it as carefully as one that says, "Dear Maurice" at the top.

Study your market. Get your letter/query to the correct person. When you do this, you've already made your query better than most.

Step 7: Promote Your Writing Business

Your freelance business is just that: a business.

You may be chagrined to find out that just because you're a fabulous writer, agents, marketing managers, and editors won't beat a path to your door. You need to make all these people aware of the fact that you're a writer.

As a copywriter, you can do this by drafting a stellar sales letter promoting your services to local businesses. Get a mailing list from your local Chamber of Commerce and start licking envelopes.

You can also write an effective brochure to send to prospective clients.

Postcards mailed on a regular basis are a great way to keep in touch with clients as well.

Scour your local paper and find businesses that have an ad budget. If they advertise on a regular basis, chances are they have a budget. See if you can get a little piece of it by writing effective copy for those ads.

Books like Jumpstart Your Writing Career and Snag Paying Assignments (http://FilbertPublishing.com) have a ton of ideas on how to promote your business.

You need to do the same thing when you're contacting agents, editors, and publishers. Contact them with a well-crafted query whenever you have a new project to present to them. Your Writer's Market should be in tatters by the time the new update is released.

And this leads to step 8…

Step 8: Send out Queries and Sales Letters on a Regular Basis

If you don't have a regular promotion plan, you won't have regular work.

Let me repeat that: If you don't have a regular promotion plan, you won't have regular work.

Decide how many queries you'll send out on a daily basis. Then do it.

Sending out one query per day is better than sending a batch and sitting back and waiting.

You get a rhythm in your career when you send out a set number daily. And never miss a day. Even when you have so much work that you can't see straight… send out your set number of queries.

Do the same thing for sales letters. If you want copywriting assignments, you need to send out those sales letters.

I send out a set number of queries and sales letters daily. Because copywriting pays better than articles, I usually send out more sales letters than I do queries. But I keep that number constant.

Oh… and always tweak your queries and sales letters. As your writing skills grow, so will your promo skills.

Keeping your promo plan regular will keep your stream of work regular.

Step 9: Experiment with Your Promo Materials

I just mentioned tweaking your queries and sales letters.

You need to do this because you never want your promo materials to get stale.

That being said, whenever you find a promotional method that works well in landing writing assignments, stick with it.

For example, if direct mail is working well for you, keep sending out letters. BUT, occasionally experiment with a different headline or premium. If you find that it boosts response, keep it. Otherwise, keep tweaking and refining to keep the response rate where you'd like it to be.

Also, experiment with new promo methods. For example, while reading Peter Bowerman's The Well Fed Writer, I discovered he liked postcards. I'd never used one before, but drafted one on my desktop publishing program. I sent out a few and was surprised at the nice response.

Postcards are inexpensive to make, print, and mail. I'm glad I took his advice and gave it a whirl.

Step 10: Always be on the Lookout For New Ideas

The main commodity we writers sell is Ideas. Unfortunately, any number of factors can affect the quality and quantity of ideas that pop in our heads.

Get too caught up in promotion… worrying about results, over focusing on it… and you may find your idea pool running dry.

Get to surfing the 'net too much… chatting, checking e-mail, trolling for celebrity gossip… and you could find your creativity decline.

That being said, it's wise to strike a balance between all the activities you need to do to keep your writing business humming smooth and actually writing.

You know you're off track when you hit a writer's block. When you can't write, that means you've allowed your idea pool to dry up. That's when it's time to reevaluate your activities.

But, assuming all is well in your writing life and ideas are flitting around you on a regular basis. That's when it's helpful to keep a notebook handy to keep track of those elusive ideas when they finally come to perch.

So… where do you find ideas?

They're inside you. It's just a matter of jostling them awake.

Begin by surfing to newsgroups to find out what people are talking about.

Read voraciously. Read until something triggers your

imagination.

Listen to conversations. (OK… don't be weird about this one… you don't want to be an eavesdropper or anything….)

Talk to people.

Go to the mall and observe people, interactions, how they react to sales pitches.

Write down every idea that flits through your mind, then go back to it later to see if it would make a good book/article/copywriting lead idea.

Step 11: Write. Every day.

No matter what.

OK. I know I said we'd talk about Ten Steps to Freelancing Freedom. Changed my mind. We're on to number 11 now….

Remember this: If you don't write, you're not a writer.

It's easy to read about writing. It's easy to discuss writing. It's easy to pick other people's writing apart (in fact, sometimes it's downright fun… admit it).

But, you would be surprised that many people who call themselves writers rarely write.

Avoid hanging out on the web too much. Chuck the computer games. Make sure your promotional activities don't exceed a set number of hours each day.

Turn off the TV and read in the evening… you have to read voraciously to be a writer… but don't let the reading time take up your writing time.

It's easy to enjoy all the trappings of being a freelance writer… the freedom of a flexible schedule… owning your afternoons… but you're not a freelance writer unless you write. Period.

Once you get cooking on a hot project, keep writing. Avoid interruptions like unnecessary phone conversations so you can keep on track.

Some writers decide how many words they'll write every day, then they stick with it. That way they have a predicable output of writing every day.

Some people are "spurt" writers who are incredibly prolific one day, then are less so the next.

Decide what kind of writer you are, then make a plan that'll work for your style of writing.

Step 12: Take Your Job Seriously

"Hey Beth, since you work at home, do you suppose you can volunteer to head up our {insert worthy cause here}?"

"Nope. I have to work tomorrow."

If I had a nickel for every time I heard that sentence (or one similar to it) I'd be a very rich woman. (Please note... if you truly LOVE heading up fund raising events, blood drives, etc., please feel free to do this... but don't take the job unless you want to.)

Yes. We're freelance writers. Yes. We have flexible schedules. We probably write from home.

BUT...

Our job is just as real as a 9 to 5er. If we miss a phone call, we miss an assignment. When we miss an assignment, we miss a paycheck.

When you're a freelance writer, you're self employed. You're a business person. When you take on an assignment you've promised to deliver a quality product, on budget, when your client needs it.

Never miss a deadline. Never charge more than you agreed.

Take this job seriously. If you do this, other people will, too.

That being said, I use a portable digital phone for all my business calls. This allows me the freedom I need to pick up my child from school, go to concerts, or just hang out with him at the Walmart snack bar (those cookies are awesome!) and never miss a client's call.

I've found ways to take advantage of my flexible schedule while maintaining the professionalism of having a business phone.

Here's another example:

During the last election, my tiny town couldn't find enough election judges. Because I enjoy the electoral process, I volunteered to help. But to be able to do this, I had to work ahead on all my projects. I contacted my clients to warn them that if they needed any quick rewrites or fast turnaround times on that day, I wouldn't be able to deliver. I also brought my phone with me in case they had any questions.

With careful planning, I had a great day at the polls, my work life wasn't interrupted too much, and I felt good about fulfilling a civic duty.

But it was my choice. And any work outside your freelance career should be your choice as well.

So... Do You Still Want to Write as a Freelancer?

Freelancing is the best job in the world. Hands down.

With careful planning, you'll have a strong idea of where you want your business to go. With a strong idea of where you want to go, you'll in all likelihood make your way there – if you work daily and don't give up.

Not working daily and eventually giving up: that's why most freelancers fail. And that's exactly how you'll succeed and blow your competition out of the water.

Remember, writing is a business. Treat it like a business and you'll find success.

Accept that you'll face rejection – a lot of it. In the beginning you'll probably receive more rejections than you will acceptance letters.

But that's OK.

Learn from each rejection by re-polishing your query. Then send it out again.

You'll reduce the number of rejections you'll receive by targeting smaller publications first. Don't forget to send proposals/queries to local publications as well.

After you've written for smaller publications, start heading for medium-sized pubs as well.

After you have a solid foundation of clips, you can keep building on your successes until you're exactly where you

want to be.
  And that's when life gets really interesting....

Beyond The Writer's Market... Finding Lucrative Writing Assignments in Any Economy

The annual Writer's Market is a gold mine of information for freelance writers. If you want to get paid to write articles for magazines, you'll have literally thousands of opportunities presented before you when you crack open that book (or surf to their website).

But as a freelance writer, if you want to make a truly regular and significant income, you need to look beyond the Writer's Market for freelance opportunities.

This section will help you do just that.

As you thumb through these pages, remember that some of the best writing assignments may not involve writing articles. There is an entire field of writing open to you that involves less research, fewer revisions, and significantly higher pay.

Writing income comes in many shapes and sizes.

Instead of concentrating your efforts on writing articles and books, turn your head (just a little) and take a look at some of the mail that flows into your post office box on a daily basis.

Check out the advertisements in the local newspaper.

Read some of the brochures you pick up at the doctor's office.

Somebody wrote those promotional materials... and got paid to write it.

When you write advertising/promotional materials for businesses, you'll find your pay is higher and the competition is lower.

If you're looking to boost your income, writing for local, state, national, and international businesses is the fastest, easiest, and best way to do this.

But how do you find companies that need an awesome writer to write their advertising materials?

It's really not that tough. With just a little time, patience, and perseverance, you'll soon have more work than you can handle.

So without any further ado, let's get to work and find some of those lucrative writing assignments....

Online Markets

Believe it or not, you can find regular writing gigs on various job boards like:

http://Monster.com
http://CareerBuilder.com
http://Guru.com
http://jobs.com
http://journalismjobs.com
http://marketingjobs.com

Just type "Freelance" into the search engine on any of these sites and scan the listings. You'll be surprised at how many opportunities pop up.

You can also search for freelance job boards. Surf to a good search engine like http://google.com and place the word "freelance job board" into it and see what pops up.

Some other search engines you can use for this type of search are:

http://yahoo.com
http://scrubtheweb.com
http://lycos.com

As you're surfing the web, you'll undoubtedly find sites that match freelancers to clients. Two of the most popular are:

http://upwork.com
http://guru.com

Please approach sites like these with caution. Here's why:

Both Elance (now UpWork) and Guru charge a yearly fee for the opportunity to "bid" on freelance projects. This significantly reduces the amount of money you'll earn on the projects you'll get from them.

It also creates a competitive environment that artificially suppresses freelance wages.

To make matters worse, depending on the economic

conditions, you may or may not recoup your yearly investment.

I signed up for Guru in late 2002. I recouped my investment. But I didn't renew my membership after the number of freelancers ballooned to over 90,000 while the number of available writing jobs shrunk to around 20,000.

I don't like those odds.

Besides, there are better and more profitable ways to find work.

If you're desperate and want to build a portfolio... go ahead and sign up for a service like this. But I don't recommend it for one big reason.

Money should always flow towards a writer – not away from him/her. If someone hires you to write for them, they should pay you. Not the other way around.

Local Opportunities

Some of your most lucrative writing assignments could be hidden in your own back yard. Local businesses need well-written marketing materials as much as (probably more than) magazine editors need great articles. You can find some of these companies by checking out your yellow pages.

Get your hands on as many local phone books as you can find. Scan the yellow pages and look for some larger businesses in your area (ones that probably have an ad budget).

Trawl Google and dig up local companies in your niche and start working up a nice pitch to help them with their marketing.

How will you know if they have an ad budget? Easy. As you're trawling, take not of their web presence, any ads they run, and their social media finesse. If you've got access to a local phone book, see if they've purchased a larger yellow page ad. If you see some activity in the marketing department, they probably have some money set aside for advertising.

Write down the contact information for each company, or

better yet, make a copy of the ads that caught your eye. Cut them out and tape them onto an index card.

Now, you need to find out the specific person, probably the Marketing Manager, you should contact.

You want to be confident that the correct person will receive your correspondence... whether it's a contact letter, phone call, or post card.

For example, if you sent a letter advertising your writing services addressed to "Filbert Publishing," there's no telling where the letter would wind up. Chances are, it would probably land on Maury's desk. He'd take a look at it and think, "Hmmmm... I suppose Beth should get this."

At this point he'd do one of two things. He'd either:

1. Get out of his chair and place it on my desk -or-
2. Stick the letter on top of his desk and decide to give it to me later.

My money's on option #2. I wouldn't see that letter for a l-o-n-g time.

However, if you place my name on the envelope, the letter will immediately land on my desk, I'll open it (I LOVE getting mail!), read it, and respond.

Get the picture?

Always send your sales letters to an actual person... preferably the decision maker in the company.

You can easily find the decision maker by calling the company and asking who makes the marketing decisions. After you get a name (and perhaps even talk to him/her), send a stellar sales letter to them soliciting their business.

Oh... and make it effortless for them to respond by including a stamped pre-addressed postcard and/or toll free phone number (easy to do if you're targeting local companies) where you can be reached.

You can also find businesses that have ad budgets in local, regional, and state-wide newspapers as well. These companies will probably be interested in making their ads as profitable as possible and just may be in the market for a stellar copywriter (that's what you're called when you write marketing materials).

When you're scanning newspapers for potential clients, once you find an interesting ad, you can do a few things:

1. You can contact the company and let them know that you write stellar ad copy and would love to meet with them to discuss their writing needs.

2. You can find an ad that isn't as strong as it can be, cut it out, improve it, and send it to the company.

3. You can find an ad that isn't strong and draft a letter briefly outlining ways to strengthen it. Be sure to include your contact information.

I'm always inclined to simply contact the company and skip strengthening their ads. I included the second two options because I know of more than one copywriter who has had great success strengthening ads.

The one time I tried it, I wound up critiquing the copy the marketing manager had written himself. He didn't like what I had to say and I didn't get the assignment.

If you decide to go the ad critique route, be sure to be diplomatic about it. Mention the necessary changes without stepping on toes.

Here's something else to think about when you scan ads for the yellow pages and newspapers: you have a bigger chance of landing a writing assignment if you provide graphic design services as well.

The fundamentals of good graphic design aren't that difficult to learn. I began my career as a writer, but have since taken some design classes. Boy... it's a LOT easier to land assignments when you can say, "I'll lay it out for you as well."

Your Local Chamber of Commerce

When you start your freelance writing business, you'd be wise to join your local Chamber of Commerce.

I know... you probably could afford those yearly dues about as much as you can afford to have another hole drilled in your head.

However, for (often) under a dollar a day, you'll have access to all the movers and shakers in your community. You'll also meet local business owners who often make marketing decisions.

In all likelihood, you'll also have the opportunity to build your portfolio by writing pro-bono materials for local non-profit organizations. If you volunteer to help local charities, you'll build good will in your community and will meet even more prospective clients. If you have the time, it's always beneficial to donate your time and talent to a worthy cause.

For example, when my husband is volunteering his talents to the latest Habitat for Humanity project, he gets the opportunity to meet a wide range of individuals... doctors, lawyers, business people... the list is endless. Never miss an opportunity to meet new people... especially people who share similar interests to you. You just may make not only a new client, but a friend.

When you're a member of your local Chamber of Commerce, you'll be a member of the "in" group. It's like having your finger on the pulse of your community. You'll hear news before the general public, you'll know what's new before other business owners, plus you'll be a member of an elite group... a business owner who cares about the business environment in your community. Everyone wins when a community has a strong Chamber.

The Arts

My community has what's called an "Arts Council." Writers, artists, crafters, dancers, and musicians (just to name a few) gather together and promote each other's work. They have a yearly fund raiser and publish a yearly "Artist Registry and Resource Guide."

Connections you can make by being a part of an organization like this can be invaluable. You just may find yourself promoting your latest book, writing articles, and making friends with people who share similar interests to yours.

Contact your local school district, city council, or neighborhood art teacher to find out what kinds of organizations you can join to subtly promote your writing business.

Referrals

Whenever you finish a project say these words, "Do you have any colleagues who may need something written?"

Ask your clients for testimonials.

Give satisfied clients a few of your business cards and ask them to give them to non-competing business acquaintances.

Word of mouth is the best advertising you can't buy. A satisfied client will spread the word more effectively than any radio, television, or newspaper ad.

Conversely, bad word of mouth can devastate your business. Make sure all the work you submit to clients is your absolute best. Make sure you've researched your subject thoroughly. Make your writing skills as sharp as they can be. Care about your client and their business.

If you do this on a regular basis, you won't have to worry about bad referrals. Nor will you have to worry about getting testimonials and great word of mouth advertising.

Participate in Local Events

You need to become the writing expert in your community. You need to become the person EVERYONE knows they should go to when they need something written.

To do this, you need to become well-known in your community. You also need to establish a reputation of excellence, accuracy, and dedication to your craft.

You do this by writing articles for your local paper. (Be sure you receive a byline.) Write letters to the editor. Make yourself available for interviews. Speak to local civic (and service) groups.

Keep your ad efforts constant. A steady stream of small ads is far more effective than one huge ad followed by nothing.

Volunteer to speak to school groups, scout troops, and other organizations. Talk about what you know best... what is effective writing, the importance of effective writing, how effective writing can change the world....

Slow and steady wins the race.

Keep your speaking engagements constant, your ad efforts constant, and a constant flow of quality work coming from your office and you'll soon find yourself making a stellar living.

Attend Conferences and Seminars

Conferences are a great place to meet potential clients. Our local Chamber has regular conferences covering almost every aspect of the business environment. As an advertising writer, you'll certainly have something to contribute to almost any discussion.

Writers' conferences are a grand place to meet editors, agents, and publishers.

You can meet the big direct mailers, other copywriters, and marketing managers at copywriting seminars.

Attend as many conferences as your budget will allow. Network, make friends, and bring a stack of business cards. Don't overtly sell your services at these events, but a constant soft sell is perfectly acceptable.

Be sure to introduce yourself to the speakers at these events. Print a bunch of business cards and distribute them liberally. You'll make an invaluable contact in your field, plus you just may make a good friend.

Trawl Places Where Your Customers Hang Out

You need to become well known to your potential customers.

If you write for local businesses, attend local business events. Dress appropriately and get to as many events as you can.

If you write books, attend events where your readers hang out. For example, if you wrote a quilting book, attend quilter events.

Become the expert in your field. When you're an expert, you'll automatically obtain a readership... and clients.

You want to become so well known that customers want to hire you... and only you... and it's their loss if you're too busy to take on the assignment.

This is easiest accomplished at the local level. Then grow your expertise until you're a regional expert... then a state expert... then... well... you never know what'll happen from there.

Write Stellar Promotional Materials

Your business card, brochure, clips, portfolio, and other sales materials must be stellar. They have to be so good, that your clients will instantly know that you produce quality work. It's easy to include all of this in a mini-promo kit on your website.

They must shine, be unique, and emphasize what makes you better than all the other writers in your community.

To make your sales materials shine, you'll need to decide what you can offer your clients that nobody else can. What makes you unique? What makes you better than your competition?

Once you pinpoint this uniqueness about your abilities, you've just found what copywriters call your "USP" or "Unique Selling Proposition."

Grab your USP and hang tight because this will be the theme of all your promotional materials.

For example, suppose you're the only writer in your area who has been professionally trained as a copywriter. Maybe you've got an aspect to your education that you can highlight. Maybe you're a published writer.

Doesn't matter... just dig until you find what makes you unique. Then use this knowledge to craft the image you want to display to your clients.

After you've decided what makes you unique, you need to think about your clients. What do they need? What do they want? What can you do for them? How can you use your USP to make their business succeed?

Let me repeat that: How can you use your USP to help your clients succeed?

You need to think about this because, to be honest, your clients don't care about you. They only care about what you can do for them. Everything you write... everything you plan on distributing needs to be written with your clients question in mind: "What will this do for me and my business?"

This means that a sentence like this:

"I graduated Summa Cum Laude from St. Cloud State University..."

Needs to be written like this:

"When you need an educated writer... someone who knows how to persevere until your project is absolutely perfect... give me a call..."

See how the message switches from the "writer" focus to the "client" focus? You need to talk directly to your reader and keep his/her interests paramount in your mind. Then write your message as though you were having an interesting conversation with them.

Sounds easy?

Well, it's not... at least for most of your competition. That's why you've got a bigger chance of finding success.

And speaking of success...

Success Comes To Those Who Persevere

Don't give up. Keep sending out your promotional materials. Keep polishing them.

Continue to do whatever it is to know more, practice more, and become so much better than your competition that clients would be crazy not to hire you.

Always remember... the minute you give up, you've failed. Every time you give it one more shot, you're one step closer to living the life you want to lead as a freelance writer.

Success on your own terms is possible. I'm the perfect example of that.

How To Write, Produce, and Sell Profitable Books
A Self Publishing Primer

Selling books, special reports and articles is one of the easiest businesses to start and operate; yet it has the potential for excellent earnings. Writing a book and having a major publisher accept it is very difficult. For this reason, many writers have turned to self-publishing. You can even become a publisher if you don't consider yourself a writer.

Why Self-Publishing?

Even if a major publisher accepts your book, it could be up to 1 to 2 years before it is actually on the bookshelves. Plus, your chance of making much money is very slim because most large publishing houses only actively promote the big name authors and hot topics. The vast majority of their books receive little promotion and are finally sold at huge discounts to the book remainder companies.

By contrast, by self publishing, you can write a book or booklet and have it printed within as little as one to two months. You can do the promoting, sell to bookstores, sell it by mail, and reap all the profits instead of just a small author royalty.

For an increasing number of writers, self publishing is a viable first step in jumpstarting their writing career. With self publishing you don't have to be concerned with acceptance by a major publisher. You can have complete control over the contents of the book, and you decide how to market it. You can choose a large print run or you can use some of the newer technologies that will allow you to print one book at a time – otherwise known as POD or "Print on Demand."

Writing A Book

Writing a book or report is not as difficult as you might think. The trick is to be organized and to break the project into small sections. Then you can complete each section separately. First, I'll describe techniques to help you write your own book. Then, I'll cover methods for having others to write a book for you.

Organizing your book is relatively easy. First, create a brief outline with a title for each major section of the chapter. Each chapter should have several subheadings. Then you can make individual folders for each chapter, and start putting your notes and research material in those folders.

You can write on note cards and organize your book that way as well. Here's how it works: Every time you run across information that will work well for your book, jot down the idea on a note card. Be sure to cite your source. Then cut out the article and place it in the folder with your note card. When you sit down to work on that chapter, pull out the cards and place them in order. Then as you flesh out the information, your article information is readily available.

Next, you need to organize your time. Try to spend at least 20 to 30 minutes per day writing. Sit down and think about where you can carve this time out of your schedule. Try to figure out where you can reclaim some lost (or wasted) time. Then have your materials set to go so you can sit down at the computer and get cracking.

Voice recognition software has been an incredible development for many authors. For example, I often bring my tiny voice recorder on my walks and dictate my latest chapter into it. While I prepare breakfast, I download that audio file into my word processing software. When I'm ready to get writing, I already have well over 1,200 words written and ready to edit.

This technology has transformed my writing routine, making my 2k words per day goal more than achievable.

That said, make sure you write daily. No matter what.

Don't think about writing an entire book. Just keep breaking it into small tasks and the job will become easier.

Research
Most of the research for your book can be done through interviews, by gaining more experience in your topic,

researching at the local library, purchases at the local bookstore, by mail, and the Internet. Be careful with online searches. Many people claim expertise in topics in which they may lack direct experience. Avoid such people, websites, and less than excellent information.

Search for as many books and magazines about your topic as you can possibly find. Read and take notes. Then place the notes into the folders you have already prepared.

Be careful, though. Like I just mentioned, make sure your source is credible. Some Internet sites contain erroneous information. If a piece of information for your book, report, or article is questionable, don't use it until you've been able to substantiate the information. You don't want to ruin your credibility because of shabby research. Take time. Become an expert. It's worth it.

Your research may uncover chapter topics you haven't thought of. Always be willing to add new sections to your book. And don't be afraid to do too much research. Gather about twice as many notes as you'll need. Then begin cutting out the redundant and unneeded material.

Do not copy material word for word from someone else's book, article, or report. This is plagiarism and is illegal. Instead, take the information and write it in your own words. Twist and mold it to make it your own. Be original, but most important, have something worth saying. Too many books are just a lifeless rehash of another book. Also, many books actually provide very little information. So make sure that your book gives some real facts that will BENEFIT your reader.

Writing Techniques

Good writing is a skill that most people possess. If you can speak coherently, you can write coherently. Contrary to popular belief, it is not difficult to learn to write well – that is certainly true for non-fiction books. Fiction and poetry are, of course, more difficult, but once again, if you can speak well, you should be able to write well enough to write a basic book.

The key to good nonfiction writing is to provide solid information in a straight forward, organized, and easy to read manner. This section is designed primarily for writing and selling non-fiction books such as: self help, how to, etc.

There are a number of techniques to help make your book more readable and therefore more successful. While this chapter cannot cover all of these techniques in great detail, here are a few indispensable tools that every writer should have:

☐A good dictionary
☐A Thesaurus
☐The Elements of Style by Strunk and White
☐A Synonym Finder

Here are a few techniques that will improve your writing.

☐Don't try to impress by using long, fancy words. Use common words whenever possible.

☐Vary your sentence length - use both long (12-15 words) and short (6-10 words) sentences.

☐Use correct English, spelling, and punctuation.

☐Avoid using the same words over and over. Instead, substitute synonyms. This is where your thesaurus can help.

☐Avoid big words if small ones will do.

☐Use active verbs and nouns.

☐Avoid using the word "I".

☐Don't overuse adjectives and adverbs.

☐Remember each chapter should have a beginning, middle, and end. So should each subsection of each chapter, and each paragraph of each subsection. This will help your book to flow in a logical manner.

The most important thing you can do is to read other books that are written well.

I can't emphasize this enough: In his book, On Writing Stephen King says, "If you don't have the time to read, you don't have the time or the tools to write."

He's right. If you don't read, you may as well hang up any aspirations about being a writer. You'll never write until you become a voracious reader. Period.

Turn off the TV. Flip on the radio. Crack open a book and have a ball.

Then get writing. Practice. Practice. And practice some more. Practice writing small reports and chapter sections. Then come back a few days later and edit your work. Read it out loud. You will soon notice your improved writing. If need be, you can always hire an editor or English teacher to polish your work. The cost is worth it.

Outline

A brief outline of your book will help you to stay organized, make your work flow in logical order, and help it be more readable. Here is a partial outline for the book Jumpstart Your Writing Career and Snag Paying Assignments.

Introduction
1.   Getting Started
2.   Make Your Writing Sparkle
3.   Writing for Business
4.   Fiction
5.   Snag Paying Assignments
6.   Never Give Up, Never Give Up, Never Give Up
7.   Keep your Journal Fresh
8.   Resources
9.   Books by Beth Ann Erickson (A Blatant Ad but an Important Section for the Writer....)

Hiring A Writer

Some people have great book ideas, but can't write or don't have the time to do it. There are other options for these people. One of them is to hire a writer. For many people, this is the best route to get started as a publisher.

If you're a writer, you very well could become the writer a non-writer hires.

Ghostwriter

A ghostwriter is a professional who produces a book that meets your guidelines, but doesn't take credit as the author. You can list yourself as the author even though the ghostwriter does the writing! You pay a flat fee to the ghostwriter and then the book becomes your property and is copyrighted in your name.

You can find ghost writers in classified sections of most writing magazines. They're also easy to find through a simple Google search. If you're a writer, ghostwriting is a viable income option for you.

Ghostwriting is widely used by celebrities and authors who don't have enough time to write for themselves. You can also work in collaboration with a ghostwriter, with you doing part of the work.

Ghostwriting fees vary depending on the length of the book and how complex the subject is. For example: fees for a 200 page income opportunity book could range from $3000 up to $6000. Professional writers with a track record can charge somewhere in the neighborhood of 12k to even 90k. Most ghostwriters require half of the fee at the start.

Buy A Book

Sometimes you can purchase an already existing book from the author or publisher. Often, the purchase price will include the remaining copies of the book at wholesale prices. For example, you could purchase the complete rights to a 60 page opportunity book for $2000, including 250 copies of the book. This may be a typical deal... just be sure you are receiving the copyright to the book also.

If you purchase a book outright, you may also want to know how many of the books have already been sold, how they were sold, and get a copy of the sales literature that was used.

Keep your eyes open for books that may be for sale. Books that are just about to go out of print may be for sale –

plus the author may appreciate having their book picked up by another publisher. Be flexible and you'll find more opportunities than you know what to do with.

Paying An Author

Another way to get books for your publishing house is to advertise for manuscripts about the topic you want. WRITER'S DIGEST and opportunity type publications are good places to advertise.

When you find a book you want, offer to pay the author 7% to 10% royalties for each book sold. Sometimes you have to pay an advance to the author. Be certain that the contract states that the book is the writer's original work. There are many other things that need to be in the contract and you'll probably need the help of a professional to prepare it.

You can also surf the net and read some of the contracts other publishing houses are offering their writers.

Once the contract is signed it becomes your responsibility to edit the book, have it formatted, have it printed, and begin marketing. In effect, you have just started your own publishing company. This method requires that you have several thousand dollars for printing the book and for marketing.

If you decide to use a POD format for your book, you can contact companies like Lightning Source and apply to become one of their publishers. If that isn't an option, IngramSpark may work.

Producing Your Book

Once your book is written and edited it is time to produce a digital copy for the printer. This copy... often a .pdf, must be just like you want the finished book to look.

There are a couple easy methods for producing a POD (or ebook) friendly .pdf file. These are:

☐ Use a word processor
☐ Use a design program like InDesign

I use my word processor.

The biggest thing to remember is to create a clean file that looks indistinguishable from a book produced by the big five.

Watch margins. Indents can be a problem. Double check everything. Then check it again to make sure it's as perfect as possible. Once the printer has the file and the book is set for production, you'll be charged for any subsequent uploads.

Dealing With Printers

When dealing with printers there are two main things to consider.

1. Always submit your file following their exact specifications. Many printers supply templates you can use to aid your formatting. Use them.

2. Read their directions. Follow them to the letter. It may feel confusing at first, but it's actually easy once you get the hang of it. Follow each step to the letter and you'll avoid a headache later.

3. When in doubt, hire someone to format and upload your book. It likely will be well worth the price if you're not exactly a tech head. The number of books that you have printed can affect the cost. LSI offers a volume discount. If you want copies to give away, it's well worth checking on this.

Printing Options

There are many other possible options such as: size of the book, use of pictures, color, and kind of paper. Surfing to http://Lightningsource.com (LSI) will give you all the information you need to decide how to best proceed with your project. They offer a crazy number of trim size, various levels of color printing, hard covers, paperbacks and much more. Ingram Spark (owned by LSI) is a more user friendly version of LightningSource. Many new writers who cannot get into LSI find a good home here.

CreateSpace (http://CreateSpace.com), owned by Amazon allows you to upload your book and get it distributed for free. It's fairly user friendly, too. Some authors find this option more than agreeable.

Finally Amazon allows you to create a print book from the file you upload on their ebook platform, KDP. This is certainly worth checking out.

No matter who you decide to print your book, always check the current specs, terms, and conditions. A fast Google search can reveal which printing/publishing company is best for your needs. Always remember, this is a fast moving topic so due diligence is in order before you make a final decision.

Copyright

A copyright claims to protect your book from being stolen. However, piracy thrives. I personally don't fret too much about it, trying to stop thieves from stealing your book is like trying to hold back water with your hand. Just make sure to include information on your other titles in every book you create. Also, it's handy to provide special downloads/gifts to people who purchase your book from a legit bookstore. Also, never forget to look at each book as the beginning of a sales funnel rather than a one-of product.

That said copyrights are issued by the Registrar of Copyrights, Library of Congress. You can download circulars, forms and other information at http://copyright.gov/

Remember to place the following information on a page at the front of your book: Copyright 20XX by (name of copyright holder). This notifies all readers that this is your book and shouldn't be copied.

Book Pricing

The retail price of your book must be carefully determined.

If you're planning on releasing a traditional-type book, head to Amazon and study price points. Find books similar to yours and make not of the price. You want your book to land somewhere in the middle zone between the lowest and highest price.

In order to sell books via mail order, author Dan Poynter recommends that you use a markup of 5 to 8 times the cost of production. This gives you plenty of margin for advertising costs, postage costs, packaging costs, dealer discounts, bookstore discounts, and still allow a profit.

A POD book will have a smaller mark up because the wholesale price per book is higher than if you ordered a complete print run. However, talk to your POD provider and find out the discount for a small print run. You may wind up with a pretty good deal.

Another rule of thumb is that it is almost impossible to make money with low cost items.

A market that embraces .99 ebooks will be a market that will be nearly impossible to earn a living wage. That said, if you use that ultra cheap book as a funnel opening and you have other products to offer (assuming you're able to contact the reader), then you could possibly recoup that loss.

That said, I like to ignore markets with such a low entry point, instead tending towards finding audiences who value great information.

Going back to markups, here's an example:

While an ebook doesn't appear to "cost" the author much because it's an intangible product, many authors have hundreds of hours invested in that title, they have editing and formatting costs, cover design... creating a great ebook isn't cheap. When they sell it for .99, they earn a whopping .35 per download.

As a contrast, a ten to one markup on a $5 item only results in a $4.50 margin, whereas a 5 to 1 markup on a $20 book results in a $16 margin. The postage, packaging, and advertising costs about the same for both books. A $5 - $6 margin usually isn't enough to have much profit left over.

However, there are exceptions to this rule.

For example some companies sell a complete line of $5 - $8 books. Most of their customers end up buying several of these low cost books at the same time. This results in an order margin of $10-$20. But for most beginners it is best to strive for at least a $10-$12 margin.

Marketing Your Book

The task of marketing your book actually begins before the book is published. This prepublication marketing can consist of press releases and free listings. Below are some listing services to check out.

Books in Print
AB 1 Dept., R.
Bowker Co.
205 East 42nd St.
New York, NY 10017
http://www.booksinprint.com

Cumulative Book Index
H.H. Wilson Co.
950 University Ave.
Bronx, NY 10452
http://onlinebooks.library.upenn.edu/

Literary Market Place
Editor
205 East 42nd St.
New York, NY 10017
Book Reviews
http://www.literarymarketplace.com

A powerful book marketing method is to get book reviews. A good book review can result in lots of sales and inquiries. So don't be shy about sending copious free review copies to magazines, bloggers (get permission first), beta readers, and reviewers.

The first step for book reviews is to compile or purchase a list of contacts. Send review copies to everyone who could give you publicity. For example: If you publish a book about using computers for business record keeping you should send review copies to computer magazines and business publications. Be sure the book gets to the correct person, either the magazine editor or book reviewer.

Here are some other important items that you may want to include: A cover letter stating why the book is important and why it should be reviewed. You may also want to include a photo the magazine can use in their article.

Include press clippings of previous book reviews and information about the author. It is also important to include a review of your book (2-3 pages) written by you. Many editors and reviewers will not have time to write a review. They will simply glance at the book and then edit the review you have included.

Always include a complete press kit on your website to make it easy for members of the media to grab information about you with a click of their mouse.

Dealers

Another useful method is to get mail order dealers and website owners to sell your book. This is usually done in two ways:

☐Put "dealer inquiries welcome" on your sales literature.

☐Contact website owners telling them how your book would be a perfect fit for their readership.

When inquiries come in, send them a package that includes sales literature, and instructions. The instructions simply tell the new dealer to place his name and address in the proper place on the sales literature. This literature can then sent to their potential customers. The point is this: Make sure you make selling your book effortless for others.

Here's an example. Suppose you wrote a fantastic love story, a perfect addition to a local florist's bouquet. You contact the florist and offer to give them a fantastic deal. Orders come in. The seller sends the bouquet. If you've already supplied the books, they'll include it. Sometimes you'll send the book yourself.

In that case, the dealer's orders are drop shipped by you. This means that the dealer sends you 40% to 50% of the book's retail price and a label addressed to his customers. Then you ship out the order. The dealer doesn't have to stock the book and you make sales without advertising. Both parties benefit.

You'll also want to offer quantity discounts to dealers who sell lots of books. These discounts can range from 50% to 60% for orders of 10 or 100 copies per order. A few good dealers can move a lot of books for you. Of course, to get a few good dealers you'll have to contend with many who will never make a sale.

Bookstores
Selling to bookstores can be done several different ways.
1. You can contact them directly
2. You can let a wholesaler (if you have one) do it for you
Bookstores normally will want to order 1 to 5 copies, and have complete return privileges if the books don't sell. The normal discount schedule is 40% and the bookstore pays postage, however, they'll want to wait 30 - 90 days before paying.

You should decide on your discount schedule right at the start. Retail bookstores usually get a 40% discount, wholesalers get 50% to 55%, libraries 10% to 20%. Some publishers use a universal discount schedule for all buyers - it is based upon the number of books purchased.

This is an easy issue to deal with. If you use LightningSource, you can decide on your discount and run with it. Most authors opt with a discount between 20 – 55 percent.

You'll also need to establish a book return policy for bookstores and wholesalers. Most return periods are for less than one year. Permission must be granted first, the returned books must be undamaged, and they must be shipped postpaid.

Again, at LightningSource, you can opt to keep your

books nonreturnable. That's what I do. Once, when dealing with a bookstore, they asked to return a group of books two years after they ordered them. I'm sure they were quite worn. I was thankful for the nonreturnable status at that point...

Selling By Mail Order

Books are one of the best selling mail order products They are easy to store and ship, have good profit margins, are easy to advertise and the public is willing to buy books by mail.

I personally enjoy mail order for a couple reasons. First, with the online brouhaha, email inboxes filling, many writers are neglecting snail mail. Remember when I mentioned utilizing multiple streams of income? Mail order is one of my favorites.

There are several methods that can be tried. Mailing out a small 6-8 page catalog of books about related titles is one good method. For example, I have seen book catalogs for: sports, military, science fiction, businesses, health, gardening, and many other topics. These catalogs are sent to people who have shown an interest in that topic. The objective is to gain a list of repeat customers who will buy several books from you.

Rodale Press is a company you should check out if you're considering selling books via direct mail. You can find them at http://www.rodale.com. Their products sell like wild fire.

Another method is to use classified ads to gain inquiries for a book. Here is an ad example: Live Longer! New Book Reveals How. This, obviously, is an ad for a health related book.

I often place online ads for the sole purpose of growing my snail mail list. A CraigsList ad (it's free) leading to a squeeze page can sometimes yield some great potential customers.

Another tip - don't place your classified ad under the heading of Books. Remember, people are interested in the benefits your book gives, not the book itself. So choose your category carefully. This classified ad method is called the "two step method." The ads get qualified inquirers who are genuinely interested in your book. Step two is to send a full package of literature that describes the book, why the customer should buy it, and gives incentives or free bonuses when they order.

Display Ads

Many companies are successfully selling books using full page or half page display ads. This method is a one step (or direct sell) method. Your ad must be carefully designed to build desire for your product, provide confidence in your company and offer some form of guarantee. If you are not a good ad writer, hire an expert to do it for you.

Most of these successful ads have several common elements as follows:

☐ An attention getting headline
☐ Description of the benefits of your book
☐ Testimonials
☐ Guarantees
☐ Perhaps a free bonus or limited time offer
☐ A clear call to action or an order coupon.

Your Web Site

You have a website. Right?

If you're a writer or publisher you need one. This is nonnegotiable. I can think of ten reasons why EVERY writer needs a website. Here they are:

1. Your website builds credibility. Having a website presence places you as an expert in your field. A writer who takes the time to write and maintain a website is a writer who takes their career seriously. Not only that, having a web address on your business cards looks impressive....

2. Your website is a wonderful place to house your clips. Every query you send out can

provide your URL along with links to your clips. Face it... a web site is like a billboard advertising your writing services. It's available 24 hours a day, seven days a week, plus it provides more information about you and your writing than any query could possibly hold.

3. Owning a website makes applying for online writing assignments a breeze. Keep an updated resume on your site. When you query online publications, place the resume URL in your query. Also include your home page. Then your site will do most of the work for you.

4. Keeping a separate page on your web site for various resumes gives your assignment searches flexibility. Create one URL for your resume that focuses on your article writing abilities. Create another one for your fiction pursuits. Maybe you want one web page solely for your copywriting achievements. Each page can hold links for corresponding clips. Creating multiple resume pages focuses your querying efforts like a laser.

5. Owning a website is inexpensive. You can easily find a reliable hosting company for as little as six bucks a month. Plus, the cost of owning it gets lower when you consider that the cost is tax deductible (if you use it solely for business purposes).

6. You can sell writing projects on your web page. Once you have a nice flow of traffic visiting your site, you can diversify your income by writing booklets, articles, reports, books... and selling them. You can even sell e-books and forgo effort of packaging items, or running to the post office.

7. Maintaining a website creates a hub where clients, other writers, and potential customers can congregate and "meet" you. When you have a website, I'm sure you'll create an e-mail link on every page so visitors can contact you. Answer every e-mail you receive. You'll make invaluable contacts, you'll network with other writers, but most of all... you'll make friends. Writing can be a lonely profession. But not so when you have your own "cheerleading section."

8. A website may make you newsworthy. And when your name is in front of your potential customers on a regular basis, you're more apt to obtain their writing assignments. What's newsworthy? The answer to that question is only limited by your imagination. Make your site the best source of information your clients need and you'll find yourself newsworthy.

9. If you want to write books, using your website to create a message board, "e-mail list" or e-mag may make finding a publisher easier. Showing a potential publisher that you've taken the time to create an audience for your subject, showing them that you've got a few thousand potential readers waiting for your messages on a regular basis just may tip the scales in your favor when it comes to considering your proposal.

10. Owning a website and attracting traffic towards it is a big step in acquiring a readership. Fiction writers will find attracting a readership invaluable. Post chapter samples of your newest project online. Request feedback. REALLY get to know your audience. You'll be surprised how your

perception of who will read your work differs from reality. When you know your audience, inside and out, you can tailor what you write to fit their needs. Then everyone's the winner. The reader receives something they need. You'll sell you're writing.

As you can see, these are some very compelling reasons to own a website. But if these haven't convinced you, here's four more bonus reasons why you should own a website.

1. You can anticipate the questions potential customers will ask and provide answers on a FAQ page. You'll save a ton of time if you don't have to repeat the answer to the same questions over and over.

2. You can stay in contact with your readers. Have an area where readers/clients/visitors can sign up for updates, news, etc. Then keep in touch with them on a regular basis.

3. You may acquire international clients. I live in Minnesota. I've written articles for people in Europe. Folks from Africa have purchased my books. I know I wouldn't have met these people without my web site.

4. You can convey the image you want to project on your web site. Want to look like a small company? Fine. Create a page that makes you look warm, cozy, and local. If you want to compete with the "big guys" make your page slick, professional, and concise. It's completely up to you.

5. Finally, your competition probably has a website and is already landing e-assignments. Know your competitors. Write better than they do. But most of all, squeeze everything you can out of every dime you put into your promotion efforts. Creating and maintaining a web site is a wonderful way to reach as many potential clients

for just a little investment of time and money. Your competition already knows this. You should too.

But most of all, creating relationships is the key to succeed as a writer in this millennium. A website enables you to create a very nice relationship with every one of your readers. Writing is a solitary profession. Interaction with people I've met through FilbertPublishing.com has become an unexpected delight as I make my way through this crazy profession.

Drive traffic to your site by writing articles, advertising in e-zines, and participating in discussion groups. Create an e-mail signature file and make sure it's included in EVERY correspondence you e-mail.

Other Considerations

The cover design of your book is important for bookstore sales. Make sure your cover is stellar.

The back cover should be like an ad that describes the benefits to be obtained from your book. This isn't the place to talk about yourself. Talk benefits. Many potential customers make a quick buying decision after reading it. So carefully choose what you put on the cover of your book.

Here is another trick used by some book publishers: They use the last 2 or 3 pages of every book as advertisements for their other books and services. Some companies report substantial extra sales from these ads.

A final earning method is from the list of people who buy your book. This mailing list can be rented to other mail order companies for $40 to $100 per thousand names. This can result in a lot of extra cash earnings. However be careful not to rent your list to people who will market products that are your direct competition. You don't want to rent your list and lose all your customers.

BUT PLEASE NOTE! Although list rental can a very lucrative way to generate income, don't do it unless your subscribers and customers give you permission to do so.

Filbert Publishing doesn't rent its list, particularly our email list, to anyone. Our customers know this and stick with us because they know we won't add to their deluge of advertising offers.

There are many other ways to make a living as a self publisher. These include: Selling related books, publishing newsletters, writing magazine articles, publishing directories, and publishing good and/or unusual fiction.

Publishing is an area that offers plenty of opportunity and earning potential. But only those who take the time to do it right will succeed.

Business Basics

Being able to perform an in-demand publishing service or selling books and related products is only part of the equation for success. There are also certain business principals that should be followed. While following these principals will not guarantee your success, they will certainly help. Here are some of these success principals:

The first step is to take care of any legal requirements that might be needed. Most communities require a business license, and states require a sales tax number. You can find out about these items from your local county government.

Next, you'll want to choose a business name that fits the type of business you are starting. Then open a business checking account in that business name. Deposit all income and pay all bills from your account. Using an accounting program like Quicken will keep your checkbook current and will make keeping it up-to-date a snap. This will be an immense help at income tax time.

Having a business checking account might also prove helpful in case you decide to borrow money. The bank where you have your account will be more receptive to your loan request.

Next, you'll want to draw up a plan of action. This plan should include such information as:

☐A definition of your business

☐How you will locate customers who will finance your business

☐A cash flow analysis

☐A study of your customers.

Purchase appropriate insurance. I've been amazed at the number of authors I've met who have skipped this very important step. Publisher insurance doens't have to break the bank and it's well worth the investment.

A good business plan will go a long way towards ensuring your success. It will also make it easier for you to borrow money if it is needed. It will also give your business direction. Too many business owners try to operate without a plan and become lost in minor details.

If all this sounds like a lot of work, you are right. But don't be discouraged. Everything doesn't have to be done at once. Start small and don't risk money that you cannot afford to lose. As your experience and cash flow grows then you can expand.

Throughout your entire business effort you'll want to read and learn as much as possible. Become both a business expert as well as a publishing expert. And always keep alert to other business possibilities so you can change and grow as opportunities develop and evaporate.

Next, you'll want to operate in an organized manner. Your business plan will help with this. But there is another method that can help you in your day to day work. This method is very simple but it works.

Whenever you have many tasks to do make a list of those tasks. Select the most important task and place it at the top of the list. Place the next most important task second and so forth until all the tasks have been placed in order of importance. Then begin work on the most important task and continue with it until done. Then start on task number two. Continue in this manner until all tasks are done. This really works!

Another important factor is that you must always strive to make a good first impression. This requires that all of your sales material must be first class in appearance. Using nicely designed and typeset sales materials can do this. If you cannot create these yourself then pay an expert to do it for you.

Next, you'll want to keep good records. Many businesses have failed even though they were making plenty of sales. They became bogged down in poor record keeping. You must keep good income and expense records for the IRS.

Also, you'll want to keep good records of your customers. For example, many retailers require stores to get the names and addresses of people who buy from them. These names are then sent to main headquarters. Then they can regularly mails brochures to their customers, thus creating more sales.

Conversely, getting your customer's email address can be very valuable, too. Make sure you receive explicit permission to email them, though. A double opt in system (through a company like MailChimp or Aweber) is essential to avoid being labeled as a spammer.

It's essential that you keep a detailed record of all your customers' names, addresses, phone numbers, and what they purchased. Then, as you develop new products, you can easily market them to customers that have already purchased something from you. Keeping good customers is far easier than trying to attract brand new ones.

Many successful business owners claim their success comes from providing more service or product than the customer expects to get. This helps to build loyal customers. It can be done in a number of ways such as: taking the time to answer questions, giving discount coupons, giving a little extra product, giving fast service, selling products of exceptional quality, and many other ways.

Always give your customers a lot of bang for their buck. Slip free booklets and bookmarks in each order. Always give them more than they expect – and you'll reap the benefits of having a satisfied customer who will tell their friends and neighbors about your great service and products.

In order to make the sale you must give the customer a

reason for wanting to buy your product. This means that you must give them confidence that you will do what your sales literature claims.

How do you build confidence? One way is to provide product guarantees. This could take the form of a 30 day money back guarantee. Another way is by providing testimonials from satisfied customers. Once you have built confidence in your company, you are 80% of the way toward making a sale.

Testimonials are not very hard to get once you have a few happy customers. Just ask them for a quote about your services, then ask for permission to use that quote when dealing with other potential customers.

Lastly, make it easy for the customer to buy from you. Accept checks, credit cards, phone orders, and perhaps even offer time payments on large items. Once you grow into a sizable company you may even want to offer a toll free order line. There are many other business techniques that will help to improve your profits. The entire point of this section is to make you aware of the need for learning these methods. If you don't, one of your competitors will and he will take the sales that you could have made.

This step is exceedingly easy with the evolution of companies like Square and Paypal.

In summation - educate yourself, read several business books and magazines, then apply these methods to your publishing business. This will give you the best chance for success. Operating a business is a lot of hard work. But the rewards outweigh the risk. Not only can you increase your income, but you can also increase your knowledge and skills

A Zine Sample

The following is an issue of Writing Etc. Editor's Note: Because Writing Etc. purchases one-time rights for its articles, this issue's articles have been replaced by excerpts from two of Beth's Books. Also, we've replaced some of the original ads with our ads. This Writing Etc. is included to give you a taste of what an e-magazine is like.

Writing Etc. – August 15, 2016
ISSN: 1545-5580
Make Your Writing Sparkle. Market Smart. Publish.
Join the brightest, most ambitious, and talented group of writers on the 'net.

To subscr*ibe to Writing Etc. and receive the fr*e e-book, "Power Queries," surf here:
http://filbertpublishing.com

Here's what you'll find in this issue:
* Writing Etc. News
* Notes from Minnesota
* Feature Article – Finding Time to Write by Beth Erickson
* Writing Etc. Yahoo
* Nobody Gonna Breaka My Stride by Beth Erickson
* Classifieds
For easier reading and red hot links, surf to
http://filbertpublishing.com

This issue is sponsored by:
Advance reviewers say:
"Writers and teachers of writing alike will find this book an invaluable resource."
"A good book and a good read, chock full of suggestions to inspire any writer's imagination."

"Thought provoking and original imagery...."
September 15... Writing Wide by Billie Williams
http://filbertpublishing.com/billie.htm

~~~~~~~~~~~~~~~~~~~~~~~~~~~~

Writing Etc. News
Self publishers re-writing scriptures?
http://www.beliefnet.com/story/131/story_13100_1.html
Book warehouse gutted by fire:
http://www.publicopiniononline.com/news/stories/200308
13/localnews/55713.html
Writing bad... and proud of it:
http://www.abs-
cbnnews.com/abs_news_body.asp?section=Opinion&oid=30
708

~~~~~~~~~~~~~~~~~~~~~~~~~~~~

Books to super charge your writing career –
Jumpstart Your Writing Career and Snag Paying
Assignments
Think it'll take forever to earn a great wage as a
freelancer? Think again. Get a complimentary Freelance
Pack when you order it directly from Filbert Publishing.
http://filbertpublishing.com/our-titles/our-
books/jumpstart-your-writing-career/
The Reclaimed Series: http://bethannerickson.com/beths-
books/trust/
E-Mag and Web Site Owners!
Did you know that Filbert Publishing has an entire cache
of articles you can use for your e-mag or website? You can
copy and paste these articles directly into your publication or
page. http://filbertpublishing.com/articles.htm
Have You Found an Article of Interest to Writers? Share it
with the group and send the URL to
mailto:filbertpublishing@filbertpublishing.com.

~~~~~~~~~~~~~~~~~~~~~~~~~~~~

Notes from Minnesota:
In two days, my baby sister will become the last of my
siblings to marry.

I was 16 years old when Janet became the newest member of our family. Totally smitten by this little bundle of energy, Janet's been a very big part of my life for the past 20-some years.

She's my walking partner... and even puts up with Lucy's (the Rat Terrier Wonder Dog) antics without much brouhaha. She dragged me to Paris back in '99. She makes sure my wardrobe isn't totally out of fashion. She's an awesome sister and an even better friend.

And now she's getting married.

I always wondered what kind of person would capture her heart. True to form, Janet created her own pathway when it came to finding her soul mate. Through a maze of technicalities, Janet met and fell in love with an incredible Brit living in Spain. His name is Daniel. Everyone he's met in Minnesota calls him "hot." Peder (my son) thinks he's the best thing to hit the states since Yu-gi-oh!.

So it is with incredible joy that I salute their upcoming marriage. My wish is that they'll receive as much joy as they give.

Have a great week everyone!

Beth

P.S. This offer's almost expired... purchase "Jumpstart Your Writing Career" directly from Filbert Publishing and you'll receive the Freelance Pack as our gift to you. Details are here: http://filbertpublishing.com/our-titles/our-books/jumpstart-your-writing-career/

Warning: On September 15, Writing Etc. will become a W-I-D-E zone. Keep your eyes on this section for details as they become available....

Now it's even easier to earn a great living as a writer – for just a couple more weeks.

Due to popular demand, you can once again receive the Freelance Pack as our gift when you order Jumpstart directly from Filbert Publishing. However, this special won't last much longer.

With Jumpstart Your Writing Career, you'll discover how easy it is to:

* Think like a writer
* Hone your writing skills until they're razor sharp
* Tackle the most lucrative branch of writing
* Learn secrets of fiction
* Organize your nonfiction articles
* Write powerful queries
* Promote your writing business for little or no money

If you want to be a freelance writer who snags paying assignments, read more here:

http://filbertpublishing.com/jumpstart.htm

~~~~~~~~~~Feature Article~~~~~~~~~~

Finding Time To Write by Beth Erickson

Life is moving at a frantic pace – at least it seems that way at my house! And if you're like me, you've always dreamed of becoming a writer. But how do you find the time in between family responsibilities, work pressures, and anything you may try to squeeze in between them.

It sounds overwhelming, doesn't it? Where are you going to find time to develop your writing skills? Well, it's not as hard as you think.

Becoming a writer with good, solid skills doesn't take as much time as you think. Just a little bit of writing each day will take you farther than you can imagine. And knowing a few tricks of the trade will advance your writing skills far beyond your competitors….

So, are you ready to get to work?

Here's your first assignment:

Take a look at your typical (if there is such a thing) day. Where can you find a block of uninterrupted time to improve your writing skills?

Can you skip a television show? Can you squeeze some writing time in while you're waiting for a bus, subway, or cab? Maybe you pick your kids up from school and have time to read or write while you're waiting in the car.

You'll be amazed at how easy it is to steal some time away from your busy schedule so you can begin your writing career.

Get out your journal. Form a loose writing schedule. Decide when you'll write. Then, just for the fun of it, write how you'll feel when you begin to write on a regular basis. And I'll see you tomorrow....

This was an excerpt from "Jumpstart Your Writing Career And Snag Paying Assignments. It's available everywhere and at FilbertPublishing.com

Be sure to nab your copy of "Reclaimed Love"
Readers say, "Another Winner! Beth Ann's newest novel will touch every emotion you have."
Here's your link: http://bethannerickson.com/beths-books/love/

Pick up any consumer magazine and you'll find them filled with personal essays. As a writer, there's absolutely no reason why you can't cash in on these opportunities to ... earn a fat paycheck... get a stellar byline... plus, it's especially easy when you know the tricks of the trade. Surf here to find out more: http://filbertpublishing.com/our-titles/our-books/101-2/

Writing Etc. Yahoos and News!
Be sure to check out Christopher Klim's newest website for writers: http://WritersNotes.com
Got news to share? Send your announcements to
mailto:filbertpublishing@filbertpublishing.com

Nobody Gonna Breaka my Stride by Beth Erickson
I enjoy reading reviews. Checking out what people are saying about some of my favorite books has become a bit of a past time.

As I read these reviews, I've noticed people tend to complain a fair amount about the pacing of a novel. I remember reading a review that said, "A glacier moves faster than this book." Another said, "I couldn't keep up with this one – if you buy it, hang on for dear life."

So how do you know how to pace your book?

Pacing is an element of storytelling that's an all-important slippery concept that sings when it's correct and can kill your manuscript when it's wrong.

Some stories need to be told in a slow lollygagging manner, while others beg to be shot out of a rifle. It all depends on the story.

For example, Reclaimed Trust needed to be breathless. A slow pace would have murdered the storyline. However my third novel, Reclaimed Hope, can't be told that way. It's slower, meticulous, and something to be savored.

So I'll ask the question again. How do you find the right pace for your book?

I've found that the only way to know if your pacing "works" is to read a lot.

Read everything you can get your hands on. Turn off the TV and read your competition's work. Make a note in the margins whenever your mind begins to wander. Mark spots where you get lost because the plot is racing.

When you finish your competition's book, study the areas you marked to find out why the story lost your interest, confused you, or made your mind wander.

Then go back to your own writing and read it. Again, mark spots that don't "work" for you. When you finish, repair the areas you marked.

After you rework your manuscript, read it out loud to hear how it flows. You won't believe how many flaws you'll find. Now rework it again.

After you're finished, let the manuscript "soak" for a few weeks. After some time has passed, read it one more time. If you're satisfied with it, give it to your first reader. Have them mark the margins with any comments they may have. Review their marks and decide which ones you'll take to heart and which you'll ignore.

Finally, always remember you won't please everyone. No matter how hard you work on your story, someone will always comment that it moved too fast/slow. Just rest easy knowing you did your absolute best and were faithful to the story inside you.

~~

This Piece is an excerpt from "Jumpstart Your Writing Career and Snag Paying Assignments" by Beth Ann Erickson

Paying Markets
Family Tree Magazine
http://www.familytreemagazine.com/gls.html
Family Fun
http://familyfun.go.com/Resources/familyfun/guidelines.d
oc
Tamarack Books
http://www.tamarackbooks.com/guide.htm
Small Farm Today
http://www.smallfarmtoday.com/writers.asp
Safe Learning
http://www.safe-learning.com/writers.shtml

Recommended Sites:
Writing For Dollars! The FREE ezine for writers featuring tips, tricks and ideas for selling what you write. Receive the FREE ebook, 83 WAYS TO MAKE MONEY WRITING when you subscribe. Email to subscribe@writingfordollars.com -*-
http://www.WritingForDollars.com
National Association of Women Writers - NAWW
Get the FREE eBooklet, RESOURCES FOR WRITERS by subscribing to NAWW WEEKLY, the FREE inspirational/how-to emagazine for women writers. Send blank e-mail to mailto:naww@onebox.com or visit us at http://www.naww.org

Swap Links with FilbertPublishing.com! If you would like to exchange links, e-mail me at filbertpublishing@filbertpublishing.com. You can see the "Writing Etc. Subscribers" page at http://filbertpublishing.com.

E-Mag And Web Site Owners! Did you know that Filbert Publishing has an entire cache of articles you can use FREE. Copy and paste these articles straight into your web site or publication. Here's the URL: http://filbertpublishing.com/articles.htm

We strive to make Writing Etc. an invaluable resource to writers. If you have any comments or suggestions, please send them to mailto:filbertpublishing@filbertpublishing.com

For Easier Reading and Red Hot URLS, read this issue online at:

http://filbertpublishing.com

The Fine Print:

You are receiving this free newsletter because you submitted your e-mail address at http://filbertpublishing.com

You'll receive your copy of Writing Etc. on or around the first and fifteenth of each month.

To receive Writing, Etc. surf to http://filbertpublishing.com and insert your e-mail address into the form.

To stop receiving this twice (and only twice) monthly e-mail… to stop receiving free tips, news, and awesome articles, simply click your personalized link at the end of this e-mail.

Please recommend this newsletter to anyone you know who'd like to learn how to make their writing sparkle. Just click on "Forward" in your email program and shoot it off to them.

PRIVACY STATEMENT: We will not distribute your email address to anyone. Ever. Period.

Please send your news items, ideas, comments, etc. to mailto:filbertpublishing@filbertpublishing.com

Writing Etc.
Box 326
Kandiyohi, MN 56251
Beth Erickson, Publisher
mailto:filbertpublishing@filbertpublishing.com
http://filbertpublishing.com/
(c) 2003- 2016 FilbertPublishing.com
The Filbert Publishing Agreement:

Sample Publishing Agreement

Publishing Agreement made this ____day of _____, 20__ between _____, whose residence address is _____ (hereinafter called the Author); and Filbert Publishing whose principal place of business is at 140 3rd Street, Box 326 Kandiyohi, MN 56251 (hereinafter called the Publisher).

In consideration of the mutual covenants herein contained, the parties agree as follows:

1. GRANT

The author hereby grants and assigns to the Publisher the exclusive rights to publish in the English language in book form in the United States of America, its territories and possessions, in the Philippine Islands, and in Canada, a Work now entitled _____(hereinafter called the Work), which title may be changed only by mutual consent in writing. The author grants and assigns to the Publisher nonexclusive rights to publish the e-book version of the Work.

2. REPRESENTATIONS AND WARRANTIES

The Author represents that s/he is the sole proprietor of the Work and that the Work to the best of his/her knowledge does not contain any libelous matter and does not violate the civil rights of any person or persons, does not infringe any existing copyright and has not heretofore been published in book form. The Author shall hold harmless and indemnify the publisher from any recovery finally sustained by reason of any violations of copyright or other property of personal right; provided, however, that the Publisher shall with all reasonable promptness notify the Author of any claim or suit which may involve the warranties of the Author hereunder; and the Author agrees fully to cooperate in the defense thereof. The warranties contained in this article do not extend to drawings, illustrations, or other material not furnished by the Author.

The Author agrees to hold the Publisher harmless and

indemnify the Publisher against any claim, demand, action, suit, proceeding, or any expense whatsoever arising from claims or infringement of copyright or proprietary right, or claims of libel, obscenity, invasion of privacy, or any other unlawfulness based upon or arising from claims or infringement of copyright or proprietary right, or claims of libel, obscenity, invasion of privacy, or any other unlawfulness based upon or arising out of the publication or any matter pertaining to the Work.

The Author also warrants and represents that, to the best of Author's knowledge and belief, all statements of fact contained in the Work are true and based on appropriate and diligent research.

3. DELIVERY

The Author agrees to deliver to the publisher not later than _____, 20__, a complete digital script of the Work. If the manuscript shall not have been delivered within three (3) months after said date the Publisher may, at its option, terminate this agreement by notice in writing posted or delivered to the Author and may recover from the Author all monies which it may have advanced to the Author upon the Work.

4. PUBLICATION

The Publisher agrees to publish the Work in book and e-book form at its own expense not later than twelve months after the delivery of the completed Work. In the event of delay from causes beyond the control of the Publisher, the publication date may be postponed accordingly, but not to exceed eighteen months from the delivery of the completed work. In case of first serialization, book publication shall be delayed until serial publication is completed.

5. COPYRIGHT

The Author, upon first publication of the Work, agrees duly to copyright it in the United States of America and Canada in the name of the Author, and to take all necessary steps to protect the copyright in the United States and Canada and under the Universal Copyright Convention.

6. EDITING AND PROOFREADING

The Publisher shall make no major changes in, additions to, or eliminations from the manuscript without the consent of the Author, and in order to obtain such consent, shall submit the copy-edited manuscript to the Author for his approval. The Publisher shall furnish the Author with a galley proof of the Work.

7. ROYALTIES AND LICENSES

The Publisher shall pay to the Author or his duly authorized representatives, the following royalties;

(a) A royalty upon the regular edition sold in the United States, Canada, and Philippines of ten percent (10%) of the retail price thereof on the first 5,000 copies sold; twelve and one-half percent (12-1/2%) on the next 2,500 copies sold; and fifteen percent (15%) on all copies sold in excess of 7,500 less returns.

(b) Fifty percent (50%) of the proceeds of any license granted to another Publisher to bring out a reprint edition of the Work.

(c) Fifty percent (50%) of the gross amount paid by a book club, whether as plate rental or royalty or otherwise, for the right to publish the Work for distribution to its members. Fifteen percent (15%) of the amount of the Publisher's charges for copies of overstock which the Publisher deems expedient to sell at a discount of seventy percent (70%) or more; provided that if such sale is made at or below cost of manufacture, no royalty shall be paid.

(d) No royalties shall be payable of free copies furnished to the Author or on copies for review, sample, or other similar purposes, or on copies destroyed and/or returned.

(e) Royalties for e-book editions of the Work will be calculated at fifty (50) percent of the e-book retail price.

No cheap edition may be published earlier than six (6) months from the date of the original publication.

8. OVERPAYMENT

In all instances in which the Author shall have received an overpayment of monies under the terms hereof, the Publisher may deduct such overpayment from any further sums payable to the Author in respect to the Work.

9. AUTHOR'S COPIES

The Publisher agrees to present to the Author five (5) free galleys and five (5) copies of the regular edition of the Work.

10. STATEMENTS AND PAYMENTS

The Publisher agrees to render quarterly statements on January 31, April 30, July 31, and October 31 each year. Payment then due shall accompany such statements.

It is the Author's responsibility to notify the Publisher when the Author's current email address and/or physical address changes.

If the Author is owed royalties and the Publisher cannot distribute those royalties because checks are being returned to the Publisher by mail, royalties owed shall be set aside for six months. If after six months the Author or Author's legally designated representative has failed to claim unpaid royalties, the royalties shall be donated to a non-profit organization of the Publisher's choice.

11. REVERSION AND TERMINATION

(a) If the Publisher shall, during the existence of this agreement, default in the delivery of quarterly statements or in the making of payments as herein provided and shall neglect or refuse to deliver such statements or make such payments, or any of them, within thirty (30) days after written notice of such default, this agreement shall terminate at the expiration of such thirty (30) days without prejudice to the Author's claim for any monies which may have accrued under this agreement or to any other rights and remedies to which the Author may be entitled.

(b) After two years (from the date written on this contract), this contract may be terminated by either party, for any reason, immediately by e-mailed request, with or without cause.

12. BANKRUPTCY AND INSOLVENCY

If the Publisher is legally judged bankrupt or liquidates its business, this Agreement shall be effectively terminated and all rights granted to the Publisher shall be terminated. The Publisher will only be responsible to the Author for the unpaid royalties at the time of insolvency.

13. ARBITRATION

Any controversy or claim arising out of this agreement or the breach thereof shall be settled by arbitration in accordance with the rules then obtaining of the American Arbitration Association, and judgment upon the award may be entered in the highest court of the forum State or Federal, having jurisdiction. Such arbitration shall be held in Kandiyohi County, Minnesota unless otherwise agreed by the parties. The Author may, at his option, in the case of failure to pay royalties, refuse to arbitrate, and pursue his legal remedies.

14. WAIVER

A waiver of any breach of this agreement or of any of the terms or conditions by either party thereto, shall not be deemed a waiver of any repetition of such breach or in any wise affect any other terms or conditions hereof; no waiver shall be valid or binding unless it shall be in writing, and signed by the parties.

15. INFRINGEMENT

If during the existence of this agreement the copyright shall be infringed, the Author may, at his/her own cost and expense, take such legal action as may be required to restrain such infringement or to seek damages therefore. The Publisher shall not be liable to the Author for the Publisher's failure to take such legal steps. Money damages recovered for an infringement shall be applied first toward the repayment of the expense of bringing and maintaining the action, and thereafter the balance shall belong to the Author, provided, however, that any money damages recovered on account of a loss of the Publisher's profits shall be divided equally between the Author and the Publisher.

16. LAW

This agreement shall be construed in accordance with the

laws of the State of Minnesota.

17. INHERITANCE

This agreement shall be binding upon and inure to the benefit of the heirs, executors, administrators and assigns of the Author, and upon and to the successors and assigns of the Publisher.

18. ALTERATION

This agreement may not be modified, altered, or changed except by an instrument in writing signed by the Author and the Publisher.

X_____
X_____
AUTHOR   Witness for the Author

X_____
X_____
PUBLISHER   Witness for the Publisher

In Conclusion

Right now, you're either so excited you can hardly see straight or you're thinking you've made the biggest mistake of your life by writing your danged manuscript.

This brings me back to the introduction: Why do you write? Why did you decide to become a writer?

There's only one correct answer to these questions. If you write to get rich... for fame... for prestige... believe me, you'll be surprised at how much work it is to achieve any of these goals. If you write because you want to live the "writer's life" of leisurely afternoons followed by wild nights of partying... it's probably not going to happen.

The only reason to write is this: You're a writer. Words are an integral part of your life... without them, your existence has no meaning.

You write despite all the rig-a-ma-row you have to go through to get your words published. You know you have a message... and everything within you supports your efforts.

You write because if you didn't, you'd go insane.

So, we writers launch forward and make our way through this maze-of-a-business, always keeping our eye focused on the prize... having the resources and ability to write our next word.

And it's on this note that I complete this book.

I certainly hope that you'll become the writer you want to be and will make the wage you'd like to make. I hope you avoid a few pitfalls along the way... and give other writers a leg-up when they've found themselves in a "tight spot."

Best of luck always... and keep in touch. You can find me at any time at http://filbertpublishing.com

Oh. And you'd make my day if you'd check out some of my other titles. Every nonfiction will support your writing endeavors and help you design your Creative Entrepreneur lifestyle.

Keep in touch!

Have a great day! – Beth

What Readers and Reviewers Say about Beth Ann Erickson's Books:

"The tale grabs my interest from the beginning and keeps me reading. This is an entertaining story, just real enough to make me think, "Well, I guess it could happen," and just improbable enough to set my own imagination to spinning daydreams." Andrea Chester, AbsoluteWrite.com

"This is a wonderfully written story about two people from diverse cultures who learn that love can be the common ground for a lot of things when given a chance to grow." Jaycee at Romance Reviews Today (http://romrevtoday.com)

Beth Ann Erickson has done an outstanding job with her narrative and protagonists. Against odds that this couple would ever meet, the love they share is beautiful. THE ALMACH is an entertaining read with an interesting premise and well-drawn secondary characters. Betty Cox, Member Reviewers International Organization (RIO)

This book is a wonderful book filled with imagery so vivid one starts to wonder "Where is Loran & are there any men like Jonathan still living there?" I recommend it very highly!! -- Penny Saltzman, Nebraska

The Almach: I was intrigued by the ceremony from the first mention of it. While the developing romance will have your heart pounding, the timely setting will send chills up and down your spine. – Rosanna Mouser, Texas

"I've finished the book it was great!!! I liked how your story line brought the reader into the book. Its almost like I could feel the sand. I'm looking forward to reading your next book!!! Junebug – A Reader.

The Almach provides ample reading pleasure and more than enough adventure for any lazy afternoon. Denise Clark for the Road to Romance

"Jumpstart Your Writing Career is a marvelous tool for novice writers and often published authors alike. It's refreshing, easy to use, and applicable." AbsoluteWrite.com

All of Beth's books are available at any bookstore and FilbertPublishing.com

Nonfiction In Print:
Jumpstart Your Writing Career (And Snag Paying Assignments)
101 No Cost (And Low Cost) Techniques To Turbo Charge Your Writing Income

The Creative Entrepreneur Series:
Publish Smart (How to Harness the Power of New Technology to Grow Your Creative Empire Right)
The Creative Entrepreneur: Insider Secrets to Effective Shoestring Marketing, Managing a Winning Mindset, Thriving in Any Economy Volume 1
The Creative Entrepreneur: Insider Secrets to Effective Shoestring Marketing, Managing a Winning Mindset, Thriving in Any Economy Volume 2
The Creative Entrepreneur: Insider Secrets to Effective Shoestring Marketing, Managing a Winning Mindset, Thriving in Any Economy Volume 3
How to Achieve Your Goals, Manage Time and Truly Live 24 Hours A Day (Editor)

Fiction:
Reclaimed Trust: Screams Fall Silent in the Desert
Reclaimed Love: Evil Lurks in Friendly Places
Reclaimed Hope: Her Truth is a Lie. His Lie Holds the Truth
Reclaimed Wonderland: Part of the Ink Slingers Collective
Reclaimed Haven: Murder on First
Reclaimed Haven: Murder on Second
Reclaimed Haven: Murder on Third

Working Titles:
Awakening The Muse Within: How to Create The Book

You Were Born To Write
  The Creative Entrepreneur's Guide Writing Awesome Ads
  Embrace Your Block

Visit BethAnnErickson.com for all the newest news,
freebies, and Beth's schedule. You never know... she just
may be coming to your community. She'd love meeting you!